THE HANDBOOK OF ANIMAL SAYINGS

Jonathan Lacey

MINERVA PRESS
ATLANTA LONDON SYDNEY

THE HANDBOOK OF ANIMAL SAYINGS

ISBN 1 85863 764 3

First Published 1998 by
MINERVA PRESS
195 Knightsbridge
London SW7 1RE

2nd Impression 1998

Printed in Great Britain for Minerva Press

THE HANDBOOK OF
ANIMAL SAYINGS

*To Giles for his ideas and
Christine for her patient typing.
To all my friends, dumb and
not so dumb, for their encouragement.
To Monsieur Marty, the butcher, for the use
of the fox and badger he keeps over his counter.*

'...languages are the pedigree of nations.'

Dr Johnson

Foreword

This little volume is not intended simply as a stocking filler or crossword aid. On the contrary, I felt it of genuine merit, when compiling it, to awaken the foreign reader's interest and remind the English reader of the richness and charm of our animal sayings. Often there is no short substitute for them without resorting to a longer and less interesting paraphrase.

More to the point, if we do not now and again 'give them wing', they will certainly suffer the same fates as so many of our animal species – slipping quietly away on an almost daily basis.

This collection is not meant to be definitive. With all the regional and dialectic variations, that would be an impossible task. It has also been kept as succinct as possible. So the regrettable omission of such gems as Dr Johnson's famous cutting comparison between lady preachers and dancing dogs.

The collection began with a few choice examples for my students of English and, in the light of their evident enjoyment, it grew and grew – which of course is inevitable in a work of this kind.

It will be seen that the definitions offered are by and large figurative ones, and I have sought to cross reference by numbers items which have a similar 'feel' to them. Some links are more tenuous than others, but the reader should feel free to make up his, or her, own mind.

Mirepoix, France
1997

Contents

Abbreviations

Aust.	Australian
cf.	compare
ditto.	the same
exp.	expletive
interj.	interjection
joc.	jocular
lit.	literal
naut.	nautical
NZ	New Zealand
pej.	pejorative
pol.	political
SA	South African
sl.	slang
US	American

Cats

1. A **cat** — a connoisseur of jazz music (297) (991); a spiteful woman (81)

2. A Cat and Mouse **Act** — a law releasing hunger-striking prisoners on licence subject to rearrest if necessary (41) (502) (1042)

3. To let the cat out of the **bag** — to disclose (harmful) secrets, usually by mistake (474) (816) (1103)

4. 'Do cats eat **bats**? Do bats eat cats?' — *The Adventures of Alice in Wonderland*. – Lewis Carroll (27) (1149)

5. To **bell** the cat — to take the first (dangerous) step (308) (1185) (1277)

6. The cat**bird** seat — ideal vantage point to survey or command (used by James Thurber (US)) (486) (526)

7.	To see a **black** cat	sign of luck (usually good in UK, bad on Continent) (213) (841) (1390)
8.	Like a cat on hot **bricks**	jumpy, restless (49) (964) (1015)
9.	Like something the cat **brought** in	very untidy (105) (486) (752)
10.	A cat **burglar**	silent, climbing housebreaker who enters by a top window (536) (716) (1393)
11.	To give a cat **call**	to whistle shrilly (64) (448) (711)
12.	Like the cat that swallowed the **canary**	very smug, self satisfied (16) (166) (361)
13.	A cats' **chorus**	loud, tuneless combination of voices (64) (230)
14.	To be a **copy** cat	to imitate (542) (582) (590)
15.	A cat's **cradle**	child's game (looping string on fingers, then transferring 'cradle' to friend) (1102) (1108) (1140)
16.	The cat that got the **cream**	very contented or smug (12) (166) (361)

17.	**Curiosity** killed the cat	lit. often used as warning (477) (1156) (1431)
18.	A cat and **dog** life	always quarrelling (34) (296)
19.	Cats and **dogs**	hard to sell products (US sl.) (87) (515) (918)
20	'Look what the cat's **dragged** in'	reference to unwelcome visitor (179) (865) (907)
21.	Cats' **eyes**	reflectors on British roads (cat's eye : precious stone) (286) (689) (901)
22.	Cat**facing**	puckering of skin of tomatoes, fruit etc. (875)
23.	A **fat** cat	privileged or 'important' person (333) (896) (1292)
24.	**Feed** the cat or feed the rat	advice to keep the cat alive to kill the rats (28) (39) (822)
25.	A cat **fight**	a brawl between women (81) (903)
26.	All cats are **grey** in the dark	all men are equal until they have made a name for themselves (232) (772)
27.	To **grin** like a Cheshire cat	lit. – Lewis Carroll (4) (36) (1149)

28.	'A man who **hangs** his cat on Monday for killing a mouse on Sunday'	definition of a Puritan (17th c.) (24) (143) (623)
29.	A cat **head**	beam at prow (sharp end) of ship for hoisting and securing anchor (486) (851)
30.	A cat in **hell's** chance	no chance at all (82) (101) (1553)
31.	Cat-**ice**	thin, treacherous ice (662) (902) (1259)
32.	'That cat won't **jump**'	reference to unconvincing idea or argument (129) (356)
33.	See which way the cat **jumps**	wait and see before committing oneself (92) (1352) (1501)
34.	To fight like a pair of **Kilkenny** cats	to fight savagely until both parties are killed (18) (1512) (1517)]
35.	A cat may look at a **king·**	reference to class equality – ('I'm as good as you are') (26) (414)
36.	Enough to make a cat **laugh**	hilarious cf. enough to make a cat talk: reference to good liquor (27) (632) (1349)

37.	A cat-**lick**	a quick, rudimentary wash (958) (988)
38.	A **Manx** cat	famous breed of tailless cat from Isle of Man (50) (862)
39.	When the cat is away the **mice** will play	if authority is absent, mischief will occur (470) (500) (674)
40.	'Who's she? The cat's **mother**?'	objecting to use of 'she' instead of one's name (62) (668)
41.	To play a cat and **mouse** game	to tease sadistically (2) (182) (671)
42.	To have a cat **nap**	to doze briefly and lightly, but alert for action (158) (169) (1428)
43.	To turn cat in **pan**	to attribute one's own criticism of other people to hearsay (1036) (1186) (1485)
44.	A cat's **paw**	one who does other people's dirty work (without credit) (510) (718)
45.	Cats' **paws**	breath of light wind on water making paw-like ripples (267) (930) (944)

46.	To put the cat among the **pigeons**	to deliberately create havoc (309) (627) (1299)
47.	The cat's **pyjamas**	the best (66) (973) (1562)
48.	To **rain** cats and dogs	to rain in torrents (180) (401) (679)
49.	Like a cat on a hot tin **roof**	jittery, over-excited (8) (71) (964)
50.	A **rumpy** cat	a tailless cat (38)
51.	A **scalded** cat fears cold water	advice to take avoiding action (overreact) and ask questions later (1091) (1193)
52.	To run like a **scalded** cat	lit. (789) (1417) (1508)
53.	To **shield** with cats	unfair activity (Persians tied live cats to shields to defeat Egyptians) (263) (853)
54.	To **shoot** the cat	to vomit (sl.) (175) (1308)
55.	More ways than one to **skin** a cat	various ways to achieve one's purpose (often used as threat) (259) (1482)
56.	**Spiteful** as a cat/catty	lit. (582) (1137) (1482)

57.	'To take **suggestion** as a cat takes milk'	gullible. *The Tempest* – William Shakespeare (44) (510) (1569)
58.	A cat **suit**	one-piece trouser suit (63) (1318)
59.	Not enough room to **swing** a cat (in)	very limited space. (origin: swinging cat-o' nine tails) (906) (951) (1230)
60.	A cat-o' nine **tails**	painful whip cf a scorpion (Bible) (201) (1336)
61.	To **throw** the cat	to wrestle (Irish) (94) (597) (1356) cf. a monkey climb: wrestling move before a throw; dog fall: wrestlers fall together
62.	'Has the cat got your **tongue**?'	inviting timid person to speak (ironic/sarcastic) (75) (914) (1189)
63.	A cat**walk**	narrow walkway, eg. for fashion parade or on bridges (58) (72)
64.	To cater**waul**	to wail like cats (11) (13)
65.	A cat's **whisker**	crystal radio set (1144) (1533) (1561)
66.	The cat's **whiskers**	incomparably the best (47) (973)

67.	A **wild**cat scheme	an extravagant or risky project (5) (308)
68.	A **wild**cat strike	sudden (unofficial) industrial action (1473)
69.	The **Kit-Cat** Club	18th c. coffee house for writers and artists (kit-cat: above waist portrait, including hands) (965) (1532)
70.	Cute as a **kitten**	lit. cf. playful as... (190)
71.	**Nervous** as a kitten	lit. (8) (49) (556)
72.	A **sex** kitten	image of innocent young temptress (eg. Bardot in the 1960's) (63) (628) (1171)
73.	To have kitten**s**	to be very nervous; to behave hysterically (8) (71) (1007)
74.	A kit**ty**	stake or winnings at a card game (761) (1289)
75.	A sour-**puss**	sulking, peevish person (62) (143) (1202)
76.	A **pussy**	crude reference to female or female organ (583) (791)
77.	To pussy**foot**	to act in a weak or indecisive way (773) (1259); to support prohibition (US) (143)

78. To be pussy-**whipped**   to be dominated by a woman (US sl.) (128) (421)

79. A pussy **willow**   tree with furry buds (catkins) (533) (673) (1061)

Dogs

80. A legal **beagle**   a lawyer (2) (502) (636)

81. A **bitch**   unlikeable woman (pej. sl.) (1) (960) (1099)

82. To have as much chance as a **fiddler**'s bitch   completely out of luck (see front cover picture) (30) (213)

83. More trouble than a bitch in **heat**   very problematic, time-consuming (677) (1429)

84. A **son** of a bitch   term of contempt (sl.) (1095) (1118) (1137)

85. A **doggy**-bag   bag for uneaten restaurant food to take home, supposedly for the dog (126) (1188) (1452)

86. **Barking** dogs seldom bite   lit. (if rather optimistic); cf. to have a bark worse than one's bite (158) (1175)

87.	To **bird**-dog someone	to take his girl (US sl.) (19) (491) (515) – a bird-dog: a keen salesperson
88.	'My **black** dog'	referring to his crippling depressions – Winston Churchill (1364) (1422) (1427)
89.	To be a dogs**body**	a slave; subordinate (211) (266) (1519)
90.	A dog and **bone**	a telephone (UK rhyming slang) (296) (972) (1050)
91.	'I felt like a dog without a **bone**'	on selling Virgin Records – Richard Branson
92.	Like a dog with two bone**s**	in two minds (33) (808) (1352)
93.	A **bull**dog	University official (850); short-barrelled, large calibre pistol (507) (1394)
94.	To **bull**dog	to ground a bull by gripping horns and twisting (US) (61)
95.	The British **Bulldog**	Churchillian image of stoic courage and steadfastness (147) (247) (342)
96.	A **bulldog** clip	large spring clip for holding papers (109) (552)

97.	As fit as a **butcher**'s dog	fighting fit, on top form (1020) (1200) (1268)
98.	To **call** off the dogs	to cease acting aggressively (1175) (1357)
99.	The dogs may bark but the **caravan** moves on	time waits for no man (derived from Arabic saying) (1180)
100.	A dog **cart**	light horse-drawn carriage (1314) (1521)
101.	A dog's **chance**	a very slim chance of success (30) (1553)
102.	To wear a dog-**collar**	to be a cleric (164) (324)
103.	Every dog has its **day**	even the most wretched people have their moment of glory (567) (1164) (1457)
104.	Dog **days**	the hot season (early July to early September) (758) (1515)
105.	A dog's **dinner**/ breakfast	a mess (9) (486) (752)
106.	'Your **dinner's** in the dog'	wife's message left for husband who is 'in the doghouse', or out of favour (128) (421) (1099)

107.	To be **dressed** up like a dog's dinner	very overdressed, usually in a flashy or tacky manner (151) (439) (522)
108.	To offer a **drowning** dog a drink	to offer help too late, or when no longer needed (cf. Dr Johnson's letter to Lord Chesterfield.) (131) (849)
109.	A dog **ear**	corner of page turned over as bookmark (625) (1026) (1032)
110.	A dog **end**	stub end of a cigarette (sl.) (519) (1075) (1468)
111.	A dog **face**	a common soldier or G.I. (US pej.) (192) (644)
112.	A dog **fight**	aerial combat (884) (1012) (1507)
113.	'We don't have a dog in the **fight**'	referring to the Yugoslav War – Secretary of State Baker (US)(553) (917)
114.	A **fire** dog	an implement to support burning logs (879) (990)
115.	'A reasonable number of **fleas** is good for a dog – keeps him from broodin' over bein' a dog	E.N. Westcott

116.	Lie down with dogs and you'll arise with **fleas**	bad company rubs off (346) (704)
117.	To dog someone's **footsteps**	to follow close behind him (182) (803)
118.	A dog never **fouls** his own doorstep	one does not normally damage one's own property (620) (1399)
119.	To **go** to the dogs	to deteriorate (usually in the moral sense) (1364) (1422)
120.	'Dog**gone**!'	interjection denoting surprise or dismay (319) (488)
121.	A **hair** of the dog (that bit you)	another (small) drink to sober you up (belief that a hair from mad dog cured its bite) (281) (1264) (1484)
122.	To **hamble** a dog	to lame it to stop it hunting (131) (1431) (1543)
123.	**Hang**dog	shamefaced (397) (773) (1503); (Hangbird: Baltimore Oriole)
124.	Give a dog a bad name and **hang** him	first blacken a man's character then he's easier to finish off (774)

125.	**Hong**-Kong dog	diarrhoea (US sl. very pej.) (1528) (1530)
126.	A **hot** dog	sausage in a roll (origin – German/US) (85) (1188) (1452)
127.	To **hot**dog	to perform stunts on a surfboard (201) (798)
128.	To be in the dog**house**	to be out of favour (usually after upsetting one's wife) (78) (106) (421)
129.	'That dog won't **hunt'**	challenging or doubting a proposed course of action (used by President Johnson US) (32) (356)
130.	To **keep** a dog and bark oneself	to overdo things; waste one's energy (270) (514) (1257)
131.	Help a **lame** dog over a stile	assist those less fortunate than oneself (108) (122) (1056)
132.	A **lap**dog	a fawning, sycophantic person (1145) (1348) (1463)
133.	A dog-**leg**	a sharp turning in road etc. cf. a dog-legged stairway (810) (1124) (1264)

134.	As straight as a dog's hind **leg**	very crooked or dishonest (ironic) (536) (1037) (1469)
135.	The dog('s) **letter**	in Roman times, the letter 'R' which resembled a dog's growl (576) (1471)
136.	To **lie** doggo	to play dead or hide (836) (1313)
137.	To lead a dog's **life**	to have a miserable time of it (119) (173) (1405)
138.	'A **living** dog is better than a dead lion'	lit. (Ecclesiastes) (450) (691)
139.	'**Love** me, love my dog'	advice to take people (along with their defects and friends) as you find them (444) (918)
140.	Too **low** for the dogs to bite	utterly despicable (US) (84) (1132) (1137)
141.	'**Mad** dogs and Englishmen'	reference to English eccentricity (244) (247) (1536)
142.	To see a **man** about a dog	an excuse to get away from boring company, go to toilet etc. (544) (778)

143.	To be a dog in the **manger**	to stop others enjoying things that you have no use for (28) (75) (623)
144.	You can't teach an old dog **new** tricks	it is hard to break the habits of a lifetime (217) (1298) (1332)
145.	To treat a thing as the dogs do the **Nile**	old saying meaning to treat with contempt (234) (1350) (1438)
146.	A dog's **nose**	drink of gin and beer mixed (278) (374) (946)
147.	There's life in the **old** dog yet	down, but not defeated (95) (342) (645)
148.	Dog/doggy **paddle**	elementary swimming style (1000) (1232)
149.	A dog and **pony** show	monotonous spectacle or speech (313) (448) (1361)
150.	'He is so **poor** he could not keep a dog'	Longus 5th c. (821) (1487).cf. dog-support supplement paid to the UK welfare claimants.
151.	To **put** on the dog	to put on airs, fine clothes etc. (a dog: a stiff, high collar worn at Yale) (US) (107) (522)

152.	Let the dog see the **rabbit**	give everyone an equal chance (1326) (1449) (1542)
153.	It's an old dog for a hard **road**	experience counts in adversity (265) (266) (1518)
154.	A **sausage** dog	a dachshund (126) (157) (863)
155.	A **sea** dog	an experienced sailor (1029) (1347) (1458)
156.	A **shaggy** dog story	'never-ending' tale with unexpected ending (288) (354) (1470)
157.	'Four times as much original **sin** as other dogs'	describing fox-terriers Jerome K. Jerome (154) (863)
158.	Let **sleeping** dogs lie	advice to be prudent and resist temptation to interfere (42) (86) (1156)
159.	A **sniffer** dog	dog used to detect drugs etc. (212) (803) (1139)
160.	A dog eat dog **society**	a pitiless and ruthless world (856) (1206) (1380)
162.	The Dog **Star**	Sirius, bright chief star of constellation Canis Major (1080) (1574)

163.	'Straw dogs'	insignificant things (Lao Tzu, 3rd c. BC) (339) (692) (1487)
164.	A dog tag	personal name tag (derived from military identification tags) (US) 102) (497) (1244)
165.	The tail wagging the dog	the lesser controlling the greater; an absurdity (218) (358) (1496)
166.	Like a dog with two tails	ecstatic (12) (16) (361)
167.	A dog tent	small low-lying one man tent (238) (1041)
168.	To throw someone to the dogs	to abandon him to a bad end (652) (709)
169.	To be dog-tired	to be desperately tired; asleep on one's feet (42) (158) (769)
170.	Dog tooth	early carvings of flowers on stone (879) cf. 'egg and tooth' decoration; sharp human tooth (canine) cf. egg tooth of birds and reptiles
171.	Top dog	dominant individual (368) (1448) (1526)

172.	A dog **trot**	steady, energy-conserving running style (238) (699)
173.	To be an **under**dog	disadvantaged in a contest; a loser (137) (958)
174.	A 57 **variety** dog	a mongrel (904) (1457)
175.	'As a dog returns to his **vomit**, so a fool returns to his folly'	'Proverbs' (Bible) cf. as sick as a dog (54) (1308)
176.	The dogs of **war**	old name for mercenaries (521) (631) (1192)
177.	Dog **Watch**	short two-hour watch (naut.) (162) (1080)
178.	A **watch** dog	person or committee that enforces rules or protects the public (158) (487) (1545)
179.	Like a dog at a **wedding**	thoroughly unwelcome (20) (865) (907)
180.	**Weather** (even) a dog wouldn't go out in	atrocious weather (48) (401)
181.	To have the **wet** dog shakes	withdrawing from alcohol or drug addiction (US sl.) (212) (425)

182.	To **hound** someone	to pursue or harass him (41) (117) (803)
183.	**Hound**stooth	a type of patterned material (376) (932)
184.	'When the hounds **bay**, we know we are in the saddle'	after mixed reviews of his First Symphony – Mahler (1315) (1365)
185.	To have a **husky** voice	to have a hoarse or sexy voice (1111)
186.	**Pug**-nosed	having a short, flat nose (after Pug dog) (1351) (1414)
187.	To buy a **pup**	to be swindled; pay for a worthless item (392) (756)
188.	Puppy **fat**	reference to a chubby child (545) (1051) (1196)
189.	Puppy **love**	young (adolescent) love cf. calf love (430) (1004) (1421)
190.	As **playful** as a puppy	lit. (70) (664)
191.	'**Puppies**'	Polish urban professionals (1086)
192.	A **Terrier**	member of Territorial Army (colloq.) (111) (585)

Horses

193. Act the **ass** and people will try to ride you

people usually take you at face value (197) (712) (819)

194. 'There are asses in Vienna who take me for a second **Beethoven**'

Johannes Brahms

195. 'The **law** is a' ass'

Mr Bumble in *Oliver Twist* (but NB. the preceding words: 'If the law supposes that…') (1168) (1293)

196. To **make** an ass of oneself

to be a fool cf. a silly ass (667) (712)

197. If you want the **perfect** ass, you must go on foot

a barb against oneself (193) (233) (953)

198. To be a **pompous** ass

a self-opinionated fool (200) (373)

199. To look for **wool** on an ass

to act the fool (231) (1256)

200.	A **bayard**	person blinded by self love (198) (361) (404)
201.	A **colt**	revolving pistol (US) (93) (1125); young sportsman (1412); rope end used in thrashing (naut.) (60) (1336)
202.	A **donkey**	a small auxiliary engine on ship etc., from 2 to 4 horsepower (1048)
203.	A donkey's **breakfast**	a kind of mattress (naut.) (274) (855); woodchip wallpaper (512)
204.	A **carrot** to a donkey	an inducement (783) (959) (1474)
205.	To talk the **hind** legs off a donkey	to talk endlessly (280) (844) (967)
206.	A donkey **jacket**	a workman's jacket that became fashionable in the 1960s (1107)
207.	A **laden** donkey travels best	old Scottish saying (255) (266)
208.	To be donkey's years **old**	very old (pej.) (probably derived from 'donkey's ears') (232) (1298) (1518)

209.	To win the donkey **race**	to come in last (249) (469) (1434)
210.	Like feeding **strawberries** to a donkey	anything wasteful and expensive (224) (378) (780) cf. to shoe the goose
211.	To do the donkey **work**	to do unpleasant work avoided by others (89) (266)
212.	**Horse**	heroin sl. (159) (181) (519)
213.	**Bad** luck comes on horse-back and leaves on foot	easily acquired, hard to lose (7) (82) (461)
214.	A **beggar** on horseback	a newly rich upstart (489)
215.	If wishes were horses, **beggars** would ride	wishful thinking leads one nowhere (336) (490) (527)
216.	A nod's as good as a wink to a **blind** horse	a mere hint gives you the whole story (hence the cliché 'nod, nod, – wink, wink', to denote complicity) (1013) (1019)
217.	A horse and **buggy** attitude	outdated, old-fashioned point of view (144) (1298) (1332)
218.	To put the **cart** before the horse	to get one's priorities wrong (165) (358) (1496)

219.	To have a **charley** horse	to suffer muscle pain or a blow in region of one's crotch (122) (131) (264)
220.	To horse **collar** someone	to dominate or control him (a baseball term US) (1334) (1435) (1448)
221.	A horse of a different **colour**	an entirely different situation (256) (909)
222.	Horses for **courses**	the matching of tasks with talents (also used as an excuse if this does not happen) (444) (496)
223.	A **dark** horse	an unknown quantity (706) (708) (1083)
224.	Like singing psalms to a **dead** horse	a complete waste of time; over-optimistic (210) (378) (780)
225.	To flog a **dead** horse	to waste one's time and energy (514) (808) (1180) (dead horse: advance pay) (naut.)
226.	'All sorts of **defects** are found out in the stable door after the horse is stolen'	wisdom after the event – *Hard Times*, Charles Dickens (3) (257)

227.	A **Devil's** Coach-horse	type of beetle with scorpion-like tail (454) (1043) (1482)
228.	To **drive** a coach and horses through	easily distinguish or defeat an argument (764) (909) (1340)
229.	'I could **eat** a horse'	starving hungry cf. hungry as a horse (259) (558) (705)
230.	'As soon **expect** to get pleasure from the neighing of my horse'	commenting on the quality of German singers – Frederick the Great (13) (578) (1315)
231.	'Horse**feathers**!'	'nonsense' (199) (242) (882)
232.	To look a **gift** horse in the mouth	to inspect gifts before accepting them (a horse's teeth indicate its age) (243) (263) (616)
233.	It's a **good** horse that never stumbles, and a good wife that never grumbles	advice to make allowances – nobody is perfect (197) (829)
234.	To get on one's **high** horse	to look down on others; to set oneself apart cf. a cavalier attitude (145) (371) (548)

235.	A **hobby** horse	a constant topic of conversation; Hobby Horse: early bicycle invented by Johnson in 1819. (844) (1012) (1420)
236.	To ride a **hobby** horse to death	to kill off a project or idea through obsession (241) (966) (1420)
237.	'**Hold** your horses!'	'hold back'; 'be patient' (1130) (1239) (1435)
238.	**Iron** Horses	Native American name for trains in 19th c. US (167) (172) (316)
239.	To be in the Horse **Latitudes**	to be depressed or listless (cf. to be in the doldrums) (386) (1422)
240.	You can **lead** a horse to water, but you cannot make it drink	lit. (279) (781) (1185) Pig-headed.
241.	**Looking** for a horse to ride	seeking a victim or a pretext (236) (272) (718)
242.	'Tell that to the horse **marines**'	reference to something nonsensical (231) (302) (748)

243.	Straight from the horse's **mouth**	on the most reliable authority (ref. to checking a horse's teeth to tell its age) (253) (427) (1258)
244.	'**Oats**. A grain which, in England is generally given to horses, but in Scotland supports the people'	Dr Johnson (141) (399)
245.	A horse **opera**	a Western movie (424) (826)
246.	The **Pale** Horse	Death – 'Revelations' (Bible) (1160)
247.	'The **paradise** of women, the purgatory of men and the hell of horses'	16th c. England described by John Florio (95) (141) (1536)
248.	Horse**play** / to horse around	play boisterously (527) (657) (1289) cf. to play the horses: to gamble
249.	A one-horse **race**	one obvious winner; a foregone conclusion (often pol.) (209) (268) (1546)

250.	'Ramm's Warhorse'	description of his Oboe Concerto in C, played by Ramm (his favourite oboist) – Mozart (265) (1115)
251.	As scarce as **rocking**-horse manure (shit)	non-existent (349) (456)
252.	**Salt** horse	canned or salted beef (US) (329)
253.	Horse **sense**	common sense (Joc.: good judgement which prevents horses from betting on people) (243) (427)
254.	Horse**shoes**/quoits	game of tossing 'U'-shaped bars at small stakes (299) (369) (370) cf. a clay pigeon shoot
255.	'Don't **spare** the horses'	order to go quickly (1302) (1383) (1417)
256.	A horse from a different **stable**	a person with superior attributes (221) (360) (909)
257.	To close the **stable** door after the horse has bolted	to take preventative action too late (3) (218) (226)

258.	A **stalking** horse	a screen to hide behind; a device to conceal true intent (often pol.) (554) (718) (1545)
259.	A **starving** horse will clean its own stable	hunger is a sharp inducement (sometimes used as a threat) (55) (229) (270) cf. hungry dogs will eat dirty pudding
260	'To **swap** horses when crossing a stream'	to change sides halfway (at the most dangerous point) – Abraham Lincoln. pej. (33) (375) (1094)
261.	A one-horse **town**	a place with few amenities (660) (1361)
262.	Horse **trading**	hard bargaining to secure equal concessions (often pol.) (764) (199) (1356)
263.	A **Trojan** Horse	a treacherous deception (53) (708) (1137)
264.	A **vaulting** horse	gymnastic jumping equipment (219) (1020)
265.	An old **war** horse	symbol of experience and reliability; a veteran (153) (155) (1458)

266.	A **wheel**horse	steady, reliable worker or drudge (often pol.) (153) (1321) (1519)
267.	**White** horses	large, white-crested waves (45) (276) (401)
268.	To outstrip with **white** horses	to win an easy victory (ref. to Julius Caesar's horses) (249) (360) (1546) cf. to donkey lick: to defeat decisively (Aust.) (sl.)
269.	'**Wild** horses wouldn't hold me'	statement of determination (95) (1185) (1382)
270.	There's no need to spur on a **willing** horse	advice to avoid unnecessary effort (130) (225) (259)
271.	To back the **wrong** horse	to trust in something that fails you (1245) (1289) (1443)
272.	To saddle the **wrong** horse	to accuse the wrong person (241) (1174)
273.	A **mare's** nest	something believed in that proves unfounded; a hoax (354) (700) (1228)

274.	A **night**mare	a bad dream ('the Nightmare of Europe': Napoleon Bonaparte) (203) (769) (1567)
275.	**Shankses** / Shanks' mare	travel on foot (ironic) (283) (699) (1343)
276.	A mare's **tail**	a group of wispy clouds in the sky, cf. bird-walking weather: low, black clouds forcing birds to fly low (flying term US) (267) (679) (944)
277.	A **mule**	heel-less slipper (963); spinning machine (1564)
278.	A **Moscow** mule	cocktail of vodka, lime, bitters and ginger beer cf. a horse's neck: ginger ale with spirits (146) (374) (946)
279.	As **stubborn** as a mule	lit. (240) (473) (744)
280.	To **nag**	to find fault constantly (a nag: someone who does this) (509) (864) (870)
281.	A **Pony**	£25 (sl.) (656) (972); a small drinking glass (121); a school translation (crib)

282.	A pony **car**	a small two-seat sports car (US) (291) (1076) (1456)
283.	**Shankses** / Shanks' pony	going on foot (275) (699) (1343)
284.	A pony**tail**	type of hairstyle (377) (759) (971); 'Divine Ponytail': Roberto Baggio.
285.	A **stud**	promiscuous, macho male (pej.) (839) (1363) (stud: a type of Poker (card game))
286.	A **zebra** crossing	type of pedestrian crossing (21) (523) (833)

Cattle

287.	To **beef** about something	to complain. cf. to bleat (280) (870)
288.	To **beef** something up	to boost or exaggerate it (156) (817)
289.	Beef**eaters**	Yeomen of the Guard (guardians of the Tower of London) (436) (602) (938)
290.	**Beeves**	cattle intended for slaughter (322) (736) (1431)
291.	Double **buffalo**	55 mph speed limit (from buffalo on $5 note) (US sl.) (282) (501) (605)
292.	A **bull**-bar	large bumper or fender on motor vehicle (298) (316) (1498)
293.	**Bullish**	aggressive (512); Stock Exchange term (sending prices up) (598) (684)

294.	To bull**y** off	to start a game of Hockey (1520)
295.	Like a bull in a **china** shop	very clumsy; reckless (312) (340) (999)
296.	A bull and **cow**	a row (UK rhyming slang) (18) (90) (972)
297.	To **do** the bull	to meet informally for music making (French) (1) (707)
298.	A Bull**dozer**	large, earth-moving machine (292) (816) (1009)
299.	A bull**s**eye	a perfect shot; full marks (370) (534) (1178) cf. bull's-eye: type of lantern; kind of boiled sweet
300.	To **fight** a bull without a sword	to be at a disadvantage; to ask for trouble (642) (648) (1509)
301.	Like a bull at a **gate**	furious or reckless (587) (1207) (1274)
302.	A **load** of bull	a lot of nonsense (sl.) cf. bullshit (sl.) (231) (242) (367)
303.	To **milk** the bull (ram)	to attempt the impossible (used by Dr Johnson) (748) (1256)

304.	Like a **red** rag to a bull	deliberately provocative (603) (835) (1429)
305.	A bull-**roarer**	primitive 'flute' played by whirling overhead. cf. a bull fiddle : double bass (1115) (1121)
306.	A bull **session**	a discussion between men (US) (420) (685)
307.	To **shoot** the bull	to have a chat (US) (535) (1535) (1571) (to bull the teapot: to make a second brew) (naut.)
308.	To **take** the bull by the horns	to jump in fearlessly; to take a great risk (5) (645) (1436)
309.	To **throw** the bull	to confuse the issue (US) (46) (627) (1299)
310.	'How can he get **wisdom**... whose talk is of bullocks?'	'Ecclesiasticus' – Bible (465)
311.	To kill the fatted **calf**	to welcome someone (home) (290) (1296)
312.	Kittle-**cattle**	wayward or unpredictable (295) (340) (1286)

313.	A **cattle** show	public assembly of candidates in 'primary' elections (US pej.) (149) (448) (965)
314.	'Three acres and a **cow**'	Land reform slogan cf. Forty acres and a mule. (US Slave Reform).
315.	A **cash** cow	a reliable investment (sl.) (409) (1056) (1433)
316.	A cow-**catcher**	fender at front of loco-motive (US) (238) (292)
317.	To be **cowed**	to be intimidated (341) (406) (827)
318.	A foreign cow gives **better** milk	common tendency to overpraise unfamiliar things (404)
319.	'**Holy** cow!'	Interjection denoting surprise (120) (488) (943)
320.	Till the cows come **home**	endlessly (1130) (1232)
321.	A cow**lick**	unruly lock of hair, slicked into place (284) (759) (859)
322.	**Mad** cow('s) disease	disease caused by feeding cattle on processed sheep remains (290) (718)

323.	A **milch**/milk cow	a source of easy profit (409) (1056)
324.	A **sacred** cow	something revered or held dear (102) (319)
325.	You can't **sell** the cow and drink its milk	you cannot have things both ways – a choice must be made (24) (1509)
326.	A cow **shot**	a poor cricket stroke, resembling a pull to leg-side (380) (390) (1344)
327.	'All behind like the cow's **tail**'	running behind schedule – Petronius cf. to kiss the hare's foot: to be late for dinner (320) (1130) (1232)
328.	In two strokes of a cow's **tail**	at once (255) (789)
329.	**Tin** cow	canned milk (US) (252) (325)
330.	Neat's foot oil	oil obtained from feet of oxen (456)
331.	'It makes a difference whose **ox** is gored'	Martin Luther (1486)
332.	As strong as an **ox**	lit. (266) (645)

| 333. | 'Who drives fat **oxen** should himself be fat' | Dr Johnson (ironic) (23) (1292) |
| 334. | A bum **steer** | bad advice (US sl.) (273) (756) |

Farm Birds

335. A **bantam**weight — lightweight boxer (approx. 51 to 54 kg) (1003) (1047) (1275)

336. To count your **chickens** before they are hatched — relying on a particular (uncertain) outcome (527) (572) (1433)

337. 'Why did the chicken **cross** the road?' — saying to denote an unanswerable question. (Jocular reply: 'for some fowl reason') (338) (846)

338. A chicken and **egg** situation — an insoluble (circular) question (337) (1167) (1500)

339. Chicken**feed** — of little, or no, value (163) (244) (465)

340. Running about like a **headless** chicken — bewildered or disorganised (295) (312) (999)

341. Chicken-**hearted**/livered — fearful; a coward (317) (406) (827)

342.	'Some chicken; some **neck**!'	his reply to French claim that England would have her neck wrung – Winston Churchill (95) (147)
343.	To chicken **out**	to retract or cancel through fear (1276) (1508)
344.	To **play** chicken	to withdraw from danger at last possible moment (308) (1102) (1508)
345.	Chicken**pox**	mild, eruptive disease cf. dog's disease: influenza (Aust.) (581) (816) (1432)
346.	'If you are **raised** with chickens you will learn to lay eggs'	old Moravian saying (116) (704)
347.	To **rise** with the chickens	to get up early (US) (355) (568) (734)
348.	When the chickens come home to **roost**	justice will eventually run its course; one's sins will find one out (1198) (1482)
349.	As **scarce** as chickens' teeth	non-existent (251) (456) (463)
350.	Chicken **shit**	reference to something absurdly easy (395) (396)

351.	'She's no **spring** chicken'	reference to someone no longer young, or past their prime (208) (739) (1518)
352.	**Trussed** up like a chicken	helpless (201) (727) (1446)
353.	To offer a **cock** to Asclepius	to take prudent precautionary steps – Plato (33) (801) (841)
354.	A cock and **bull** story	an unbelievable account (156) (273) (1470)
355.	At cock **crow**	first thing in the morning (530) (568) (734)
356.	'That cock won't **crow**'	reference to an unconvincing excuse or argument (32) (129) (748)
357.	To cock an **eye** at	to give a knowing look (478) (771)
358.	Cock**eyed**	lopsided or impractical (165) (218) (1070) cf. a cockeyed bob: a sudden cyclone (Aust.)
359.	To live like **fighting** cocks	to live in luxury (724) (1329) (1442)
360.	To knock into a cocked **hat**	to outclass (256) (268)

361.	Cock-a-**hoop**	triumphant, gleeful (12) (16) (166)
362.	'A cock has great **influence** on his own dunghill'	Publilius Syrus (642) (1448)
363.	Cock-a-**leekie**	'Scotch broth' (type of soup) with leeks (459) (1375)
364.	To cock something up/to **make** a cock up	to get it completely wrong (745) (825) (1359)
365.	A **Molotov** Cocktail	a home-made petrol bomb in a bottle (624) (672) (989)
366.	A cock**pit**	pilot's place in aircraft; cramped space (467) (884) (1012)
367.	**Poppy**cock	nonsense (302) (728) (1312)
368.	Cock of the **rock**/ walk	dominant person whatever the situation (171) (1415) (1448)
369.	To take a cock **shot** at	to make a wild throw (299) (370) (564)
370.	A cock**shy**	a target to be thrown at (254) (299)

371.	To cock a **snook** at	to regard disdainfully (a snook: a nose) (234) (566) (574)
372.	To **spatch**cock a thing	to insert it in middle (sandwich fashion) – hence a chicken split open and grilled(402) (496) (753)
373.	Cock**sure**	irritatingly self-confident (198) (1200) (1219)
374.	A cock**tail**	alcoholic drink made up of a mixture of others (278) (1946); a non-thoroughbred racehorse (280) (984)
375.	A **weather**cock	a person who changes allegiance easily; turncoat (260) (626) (1095)
376.	**Duck**	strong linen or cotton material (ducks: trousers made of this); an amphibious truck (183) (618)
377.	Duck's **Arse** or D.A.	hair-style favoured by 'Teddy Boys' in the 1950s (284) (759) (971)
378.	Like water off a duck's **back**	ineffectual cf. thick-skinned (210) (224) (683)

379.	A **Bombay** Duck	dried fish usually eaten with curried dishes (South Asia) (550) (1384) (1479)
380.	To **break** one's duck	to succeed after several failures (orig.: game of cricket) (326) (1344)
381.	A **dead** duck	a failure (390) (424) (1252)
382.	Ducks' **disease**	reference to short or waddling person (pej.) (188) (551) (1051)
383.	To duck and **dive**	to try to avoid responsibility (571) (893) (983)
384.	To play ducks and **drakes**	to skim stones on water; to commit waste (210) (369) (780)
385.	To give someone a **ducking**	to push him underwater (394) (1152) (1182)
386.	Like a **dying** duck in a thunderstorm	pathetic, because, normally it would be in its element (239) (400) (1511)
387.	A Duck's **Foot**	optional key mechanism on French Horns (a hornpipe: a lively dance) (1104) (1121)

388.	A **lame** duck	weak or disabled person or object; anything seen as useless or ineffectual (131) (557) (1252)
389.	A Duck-**mole**	a Platypus (Australia) (638) (699)
390.	**Out** for a duck	failing to score in a game (specifically Cricket) (326) (1344) cf. a goose egg: zero score (US)
391.	To duck **out** of something	to avoid it (258) (983) (1108)
392.	To **half** sell someone a duck	to swindle or deceive him (French) (187) (1281) (1481)
393.	A **sitting** duck	an unmissable target (557) (564) (1304)
394.	To duck **someone**	to push his head under water (385) (657) (674)
395.	Duck **soup**	anything absurdly simple (US) (350) (373)
396.	'Can a duck **swim**?'	reference to something patently obvious (350) (373)
397.	To look like a duck in **thunder**	utterly miserable or depressed (Irish) (128) (1422)

398.	As **tight** as a duck's rump (arse)	exceedingly mean (1063) (1113) (1162)
399.	An **ugly** duckling	plain, but likely to improve with age (188)
400.	To take to something like a duck to **water**	to be in one's element (588) (751) (919)
401.	Nice **weather** for ducks	wet and windy weather (48) (180) cf. Roaring Forties: ocean areas noted for high winds
402.	To dress a **fowl**	to prepare a farm bird for cooking (372) (449) (1406)
403.	To have a **gander**	to take a look (478)
404.	To treat all one's **geese** as swans	to portray one's defects as merits (200) (373); to overvalue one's children (419)
405.	A goose**berry**	extra person accompanying a couple; person who feels left out (formerly called 'the blind dragon')(1453)
406.	Not saying '**boo**' to a goose	excessively timid (317) (343) (827)
407.	To **cook** someone's goose	to ruin him or spoil his chances (122) (1506)

408.	Goose **flesh**/pimples	skin bristling from cold or fright (31) (410) (662)
409.	To kill the goose that lays the **golden** egg	to lose future profit or benefit through present greed (315) (323) (1187)
410.	To feel a goose walking on your **grave**	to have a nasty premonition (7) (408)
411.	The old **grey** goose is dead	reporting on the death of an old mutual friend (1324) (1418)
412.	The goose **hangs**/ flies high	saying to denote all is well with the world (511) (877) (947)
413.	The **Royal** Game of Goose	very old kind of board game (mentioned by Goldsmith) (560) (1140)
414.	What's **sauce** for the goose is sauce for the gander	formula for sexual equality (35) (744)
415.	As **silly** as a goose	lit. (532) (812) (1225)
416.	To goose **someone**	to fondle or prod someone's bottom (US) (1004) (1421)

417.	The Goose-**Step**	formal, high-stepping march associated with military regimes (982) (1328)
418.	A **wild** goose chase	something that is pointless because much too difficult and not worth the trouble (514) (1117) (1553)
419.	Like a **hen** with (only) one chick	overprotective cf. like a mother hen (404) (912) (1203)
420.	A hen **party**	party for women only, usually before a wedding (306) (685)
421.	To be hen-**pecked**	to be dominated by a female (78) (106) (128)
422.	Mad as a **wet** hen	furious (US) (301) (1201) (1274)
423.	'You're a **rooster** one day; a feather duster the next'	Anon. (505) (1298) (1518)
424.	A **turkey**	unsuccessful play or film – hence 'to stuff (denigrate) a turkey' (448) (830); three consecutive strikes in tenpin bowling (254)

425.	**Cold** turkey	abstaining at once, rather than gradually – often used about drug-addiction (181) (212)
426.	A **couch** turkey	a psychoanalyst (US) (88) (1364) (1422)
427.	To **talk** turkey	to talk seriously (243) (253)
428.	Turkey **work**	type of English knot-pile needlework found on chairs, cushions etc.

Other Birds

429. An **albatross**

a burdensome, bad-luck bird (213) (461); three strokes under par on a hole in golf (452) (498)

430. The birds and the bees

explanation of the facts of life (189) (1421)

431. A **Bell**-bird

a bird with a bell-like call; a fraud (Aust.) (457) (1210)

432. To be bird-**brained**

stupid; small minded (591) (1266) (1567)

433. A mouth like a bird**cage** bottom

reference to bad language or bad breath (927); birdcage: area for parading race-horses; secondhand car-dealer's yard) (Aust.)

434. 'Always leave the bird**cage** open, lest the bird return'

Oriental saying (775) (828) (a cage without birds: 'Corsica' – Mussolini)

435.	'Playing a birdcage with a toasting fork'	describing the harpsichord – Sir Thomas Beecham (681)
436.	The Birdcatcher	British Regiment (289) (585) (938)
437.	Not a dicky-bird	not the slightest thing (1016) (1074)
438.	To do bird	to serve a term in prison (453) (468) (1230)
439.	A dolly bird	a woman dressed up to attract men (439) (522) (630)
440.	The early bird catches the worm	lit. early preparations usually bring results (568) (734)
441.	To eat like a bird	to eat very little. cf. to peck at one's food (1409) (1416)
442.	Bird's Eye	a kind of tobacco (767) (1468); type of highly prized maple wood (496) (546)
443.	A bird's eye / worm's eye view	as seen from above / below (1292)
444.	Birds of a feather flock together	similar people tend to attract, and stay with, each other (139) (815) (1330)

445.	Fine **feathers** don't make fine birds	outward appearances need not be conclusive (522) (717) (586)
446.	The bird has **flown**	reference to escape of a wanted person (453) (1229) (1346)
447.	As **free** as a bird	blithe and carefree (412) (511) (1011)
448.	To **get** the bird	to be booed (usually said of performers) (11) (149) (424)
449.	**Gospel** bird	chicken eaten on Sunday (US) (372) (402)
450.	A bird in the **hand** is worth two in the bush	something now is better than the chance of more later (138) (691) (1406)
451.	A **home** bird	a home-loving person (475) (1296)
452.	A Bird**ie**	a score of one under par on a hole in golf (471) (497) (498)
453.	A **jail**bird	a prison inmate (446) (468) (1230)
454.	A **Lady**bird	a small beetle, usually red with black spots (227) (1043)

455.	A **love** bird	an amorous person; small green parrot (1043) (1358)
456.	'Rarer than birds' **milk**'	non-existent – Aristophanes (251) (349) (to go for pigeon's milk: to go on a fool's errand)
457.	A **Mocking** bird	a bird that imitates songs of others – so person who mimics other people's voices (US) (14) (431) (542)
458.	A bird's **nest**	a ball landing in deep rough (golf) (1310) (1344)
459.	Birds' **nest** soup	soup made from swallows' nests (a Chinese delicacy) (363)
460.	A **night** bird	a person at his best at night (540) (1513)
461.	A bird of ill-**omen**	anything that brings bad luck (213) (429) (659)
462.	A bird of **passage**	person who never stays long in one place (1037)
463.	A **rare** bird	something very unusual – from Latin: 'rara avis' (349) (456) (576)
464.	A **Secretary** Bird	a snake-eating bird (SA)

465.	**Strictly** for the birds	trivial things for simple-minded people (310) (339)
466.	To kill **two** birds with one stone	to achieve two aims at once; to economise (366) (884) (1507)
467.	A **whirly**bird	a helicopter (366) (884)
468.	A **booby** hatch	a prison, mental home or similar confining place (US pej.) (Booby – seabird ungainly when on land.) (438) (453) (1230)
469.	A booby **prize**	consolation prize for last or lowest competitor (209) (249) (1434)
470.	A booby **trap**	a bucket of water etc. balanced on door-top to fall on first-comer (39) (674) (732)
471.	A **Buzzard**	a score of two over par on a hole in golf (452) (497) (498)
472.	An old **buzzard**	an irritable old person (usually male) (81) (960) (1220)
473.	A Rocky Mountain **canary**	a mule (US) (279) (504)

474.	To sing like a **canary**	to inform on others; to have a 'loose tongue' (3) (554) (1186)
475.	'No more natural than a cage... to a **cockatoo**'	on 'home life' – George Bernard Shaw (451) (923) (925)
476.	Bald as a **coot**	completely bald-headed cf. bald as a badger's 'bum' (believed source of shaving-brushes) (520) (859)
477.	A **crane**	mechanical hoist (766) (1050); boom for mounting cinema cameras (826)
478.	To **crane** one's neck	to stretch one's neck; to peer (17) (357) (403)
479.	To **crow** over something	to exult (166) (361)
480.	A crow**bar**	long, split-ended tool for levering (680) (1221)
481.	'**Breed** crows and they'll peck your eyes out'	caution to raise children well (404) (696) (1166)
482.	'When the crow's **crowing**, it's time to do your sowing'	old agricultural saying (492) (1410)

483.	To **eat** crow	to grovel; to swallow one's pride (1145) (1248)
484.	Crows' **feet**	small wrinkles around the eyes (875) cf. crow-foots: buttercups
485.	As the crow **flies**	in a straight line (974)
486.	A crow's **nest**	a place for look-out man on ship (6) (526); a complete mess (9) (752)
487.	A **scare**crow	a stuffed straw figure put in field to scare away birds (178) (1487)
488.	'**Stone** the crows!'	Interjection to express surprise (120) (319) (943)
489.	'An **upstart** crow beautified with our feathers'	Greene accusing Shakespeare of profiting from other writers and their material (214) (575) (690)
490.	Cloud-**cuckoo** land	ideal dream world (pej.) (215) (273)
491.	A cuckoo in the **nest**	an adulterous person; interloper cf. to cuckold someone: to sleep with his partner (87) (491) (1363)
492.	Cuckoo's **oats**	oats sown after April 14th (482) (1410)

493.	Dead as a **dodo**	completely dead (738) (804) (933)
494.	A **dove**	a peaceful person (pol.) (512) (770)
495.	To flutter the dove**cotes**	to get quiet people excited (1214) (1299)
496.	To dove**tail** in	to slot together snugly (carpentry term) (222) (546) (1209)
497.	An **Eagle**	a score of two strokes under par on a hole in golf (452) (471); a $10 gold coin (withdrawn 1934) (922); full colonel's insignia (US) (164)
498.	A **Double** Eagle	a score of three strokes under par on a hole in golf (also called an albatross) (452) (471) (497)
499.	Eagle-**eyed**	lit. (516) (655)
500.	To keep an eagle **eye** on someone	to watch him for any misdeeds (39) (720)
501.	When the eagle **flies**	pay-day (reference to the eagle on banknotes) (US) (291) (491)
502.	A **legal** eagle	a lawyer (2) (80) (636)

503.	**Spread**-eagled	with arms and legs spread apart (727) (1110); ('Spread-eaglism': noisy nationalism, US) (512)
504.	Eagle**stone**	clay ironstone nugget thought to have magical properties (found in eagles' nest) (473) (1142)
505.	**Egret**	down or fluff of dandelion or thistle (after type of heron with long, white tail feathers)(423) (1424)
506.	**E.M.U.**	European Monetary Union (281) (656); (emu: optimist who picks up discarded betting slips (Aust.)) (1289)
507.	A **fowl**ing piece	a light gun (93) (1394)
508.	A **gannet**	greedy person (after reputed greed of sea bird) (558) (749) (1476)
509.	To **grouse**	to complain (280) (870)
510.	To **gull** someone	to dupe or fool him (44) (1342) (1440)
511.	**Halcyon** days	carefree, happy times (a halcyon – a kingfisher) (412) (751) (1011)

512.	A **Hawk**	aggressive person (pol.) (293) (494) (503); small, hand-held board for carrying plaster to walls, ceilings etc. (203) (901)
513.	To **hawk**	to clear one's throat noisily (1274) (1311)
514.	To hawk at **eagles** with a dove	a pointless exercise, twice over (130) (225) (270)
515.	A haw**ker**	a door to door salesperson or street trader (19) (87) (1445)
516.	Hawk-**eyed**	lit. (499) (500) (655)
517.	Unable to tell a hawk from a **handsaw**	ignorant or unobservant (1225) (1327)
518.	Hash House **Harriers**	well-known international trail runners (810) (935) (1455)
519.	A **jay**	a marijuana cigarette (US sl.) (110) (212) (1075)
520.	As naked as a jay**bird**	nude (jays are born without any down on their bodies) (476) (1170)
521.	A Jay**hawker**	a ruthless, guerrilla fighter (US) (176) (631) (1192)

522.	A **Popin**jay	a gaudily dressed, loud-mouthed show-off (107) (439) (1114)
523.	A jay**walker**	pedestrian who wanders into road when not supposed to (a jay: old word for country yokel unused to road traffic) (286) (549) (833)
524.	'Go fly your **kite**'	alternative form of 'get lost' (895) (1489)
525.	As **high** as a kite	elated, eg. from drink (166) (847); or drugs (181) (212)
526.	**Kites**	topmost sails of ship (486) (851) (1347)
527.	To **lark** about	to frolic about (215) (248) (657)
528.	To **do** something for a lark	engaging in silly amusement – occasionally getting out of hand (470) (657) (1349)
529.	A **mud**lark	street child (565) (1057)
530.	To **rise** with the lark	to be up very early (355) (568) (1218)
531.	As happy as a **sky**lark	completely carefree (166) (361) (511)

532.	As crazy as a **loon**	lit. (Loon: diving bird rather unstable on land) (415) (812) (1527)
533.	A **Macaw** tree	ornamental palm tree (after exotic bird) cf. a feather palm (79) (673)
534.	A **Magpie**	a 'hit' in rifle shooting (299) (1178); obsessive collector (854) (867)
535.	To chatter like **magpies**	to talk trivia non-stop and simultaneously (307) (1535) (1571)
536.	A **Nightingale**	a type of skeleton key or hook used by locksmiths and burglars (origin: French) (10) (134)
537.	'Let me die eating **Ortolans** to the sound of soft music'	– Benjamin Disraeli (Ortolan: garden bunting (bird) called a bobolink in US)
538.	To be an **ostrich**	to deliberately ignore the truth or evade an issue (553) (1327) (1439)

539.	To take **owls** to Athens	to engage in a pointless action (owls representing wisdom and Athens being the seat of wisdom) (108) (210)
540.	A **night** owl	person habitually late to bed (owl-light: dusk, twilight) (460) (1513)
541.	As **solemn**/wise as an owl	lit. (from their immobility and facial expression) (610) (658) (762)
542.	To **parrot** something/parrot fashion	to repeat something without really understanding (14) (457) (590)
543.	As **sick** as a parrot (with a rubber beak)	frustrated or unfulfilled (1364) (1422)
544.	To **strangle** a parrot	to go for a pee (urinate) (sl.) (142) (778)
545.	As plump as a **partridge**	lit. (23) (188)
546.	**Partridge** wood	a tropical hardwood used for cabinet work (S. America, W. Indies) (442) (496) (1209)
547.	To **peacock** land	to select best plots, thereby devaluing the rest (Aust.) (772) (838) (1339)

548.	As proud as a **peacock**	lit. cf. to strut like... (234) (489)
549.	A **Pelican** crossing	a pedestrian road crossing with an audible bleep (286) (523)
550.	A Spithead **pheasant**	a kipper (naut.) (Ironic) (379) (936)
551.	**Pigeon** chested/toed	having a chest that is puffed out/toes that point inwards (382) (755) (811)
552.	To pigeon**hole** an item	to file it away for future reference (96) (607) (997)
553.	That's not **my** pigeon	not my problem or concern (113) (538) (917)
554.	A **stool** pigeon	an informer or decoy (records show that pigeons with eyes stitched up were used as lures) (258) (474)
555.	The Pigeon **Wing**	type of dance in which feet are 'clapped' together (629) (991); a 'figure' in skating (798)

556.	To **quail**	to be very afraid (71) (827) (1007)
557.	'Censure acquits the **raven**, but pursues the dove'	the weak are a 'softer' target than the strong – Juvenal 1st c. BC. (388) (393)
558.	To be **ravenous**	to be very hungry, voracious (229) (508)
559.	A Round **Robin**	a petition (originally signed in a circle to conceal order of signing) from 'rond ruban'; now sports term: each team plays all others (1084) (1441)
560.	A **Rook**	a chess piece in shape of castle cf. a knight (horse) (413) (1140)
561.	A **rookie**	a novice (189) (430)
562.	To rook **someone**	to cheat him (510) (1566) (1569)
563.	To **shag** someone	crude term for making love (sl.) (76) (455) (1441)
564.	To **snipe** at someone	to attack him from a hidden position (with bullets or verbally) (369) (393) (1079)
565.	A gutter**snipe**	a street urchin (529) (821) (1057)

566.	As cocky as a **sparrow**	cheeky or daring (sparrow-legged: having skinny legs) (369) (371) (1011)
567.	'There is a special providence in the **fall** of a sparrow'	*Hamlet* – Shakespeare (103)
568.	At sparrow's **fart**	at first light (sl.) (530) (568) (734)
569.	Sparrow **grass**	asparagus
570.	A visit from the **stork**	the birth of a baby (955) (857) (1324) (the goose month: the laying in month for women)
571.	A **swallow** dive	a shallow swimming dive (148) (388) (577)
572.	One swallow doesn't make a **summer**	advice not to be preemptive in making assumptions (336) (593) (807)
573.	A swallow-**tail**	man's formal evening coat (834) (1222) cf. a magpie-tail; type of butterfly (1150)
574.	To **swan** around	to behave regally or selfishly (234) (371) (1288)
575.	The Swan of **Avon**	William Shakespeare (489) (690)

576.	'A rare bird on this earth, like nothing so much as a **black** swan'	– Juvenal (in Roman times, black swans were thought not to exist) (349) (456) (915)
577.	A swan **dive**	type of swimming dive (571) (948)
578.	'Swans **sing** before they die – t'were no bad thing should certain persons die before they sing'	– S.T. Coleridge (230)
579.	A swan **song**	a final, culminating achievement (1497)
580.	Swan-**upping**	official head count of River Thames swans (336) (1124)
581.	Thrush	a fungal infection (345) (887) (1432)
582.	**Tit** for tat	retaliation; rhyming slang for 'hat' – so a 'titfer' (hat) (original expression was 'tip for tap') (14) (56) (1482)
583.	**Tits**	woman's breasts (from 'teats') (sl.) (76); (a tit: a worn out horse) (1374)

584. A culture **vulture**   a seeker of 'high culture'
                              (646) (1251)

585. A **Wren**   a member of the Women's
                             Royal Navy (192) (436)
                             (702)

Wild Animals

586. 'Apes are apes though clothed in scarlet'

lit. One cannot disguise one's true nature – Francis Bacon 17th c. (445) (641) (750)

587. To **go** ape

to run berserk (US sl.) (301) (603)

588. To **go** ape over something

to be wildly enthusiastic (US) (985) (1208)

589. Ape **hangers**

long motorcycle handlebars

590. To ape **someone**

to imitate or mimic his actions (14) (542)

591. 'I am a **bear** of very little brain'

character of Winnie the Pooh – created by A.A. Milne (432) (697) (1266)

592. A bear **cage**

a police station (US) (438) (468) (1230)

593. '**Catch** your bear before you sell its skin'

lit. (336) (807) (1091)

594.	To **feed** the bears	to pay a road traffic fine (US) (291) (605) (1456)
595.	A bear **garden**	a disorderly place or meeting (486) (1495)
596.	The Bear **Garden**	large, busy chamber in Royal Courts of Justice, London (80) (636) (1042)
597.	A bear **hug**	a wrestling embrace (61); a form of greeting popular in Russia (311) (645)
598.	Bear**ish**	Stock Exchange term (speculating for a fall in price) (293) (1684)
599.	To be **loaded** for bear	to be ready for aggressive action (US sl.) (603) (1274) (1568)
600.	A **mama** bear	a policewoman (US sl.) (592) (594) (1430) cf. a 'pig' (UK), a 'chicken' (France) (very pej.)
601.	'When a **man's** a bear, he's generally pretty independent'	*Nicholas Nickleby* – Charles Dickens (603) (725)
602.	A Bear**skin**	type of military headgear (289) (436) (791)

603.	Like a bear with a **sore** head	dangerously irritable (304) (601) (1087)
604.	A **teddy** bear	child's cuddly toy (named after Pres. 'Teddy' Roosevelt) (188) (857) (940)
605.	A bear **trap**	police speed trap (US sl.) (291) (594) (1383)
606.	**Woolly** bears	types of furry caterpillars (1150)
607.	A **cubby**-hole	a snug place, often kept secret or private (552) (997)
608.	**Elephant's** Foot	food plant; bread (S. Africa)
609.	As **honest** as an elephant	lit. (Anglo-Indian) (134) (645)
610.	To have the **memory** of an elephant	lit. cf. an elephant never forgets (541)
611.	To **see** the elephant	to experience life, see the 'big, wide' world (US) (947) (1492)
612.	To **see** pink elephants	to have drunken hallucinations (831) (1567)

613.	'The Great **She**-Elephant'	description of Margaret Thatcher – Dennis Healey (770) (1148)
614.	The Elephant's **Trunk**	Khartoum (because of its shape) (1097)
615.	An elephants' **wedding**	a merger between two giant companies (633) (952) (1322)
616.	A **white** elephant	a useless object; a drain on one's resources (originally in form of an unwanted gift) (232) (388)
617.	'**Wild** elephants are caught by tame; with money it is just the same'	– Bidpai, 4th c BC. cf. a rogue elephant: a rebel (783) (959) (1131)
618.	Ferret	cotton or silk tape (376) (686)
619.	To **ferret** something out	to discover by persistence (962) (1162)
620.	The clever **fox** avoids his neighbours' hens	lit. One does not create trouble in one's own backyard (118) (1399)
621.	As **cunning** as a fox	lit. cf. to outfox (658) (1035)

622.	A **flying** fox	a large, fruit-eating bat (Aust.) (785)
623.	'The fox, when he cannot reach the **grapes**, says they are not ripe'	– George Herbert, 17th c., after Aesop (hence 'sour grapes') (28) (143)
624.	A fox**hole**	a small trench for one or two soldiers (365) (989) (1079)
625.	Fox**ing**	brown spots on paper due to ageing (109) (1026)
626.	To **run** with the fox/hare and hunt with the hounds	to be two-faced; to back both sides (260) (375) (1306)
627.	To **set** the fox to keep the geese	to ask for trouble (46) (309) (714)
628.	A **stone** fox	an attractive woman (72) (439)
629.	The Fox**trot**	a type of dance (in double time) (555) (991) (1000) cf. the Turkey Trot: ragtime one-step
630.	Fox**y**	cunning (658) (1035); sexually alluring (439)

631.	A **gorilla**	a bodyguard; tough, ill-tempered person (176) (521) (1205)
632.	To laugh like a **hyena**	to laugh uproariously (36) (1349)
633.	A **jumbo**	anything unusually big (origin 'Jumbo' – name of first African elephant exhibited in England in 1865) (615) (1068)
634.	**Mumbo**-jumbo	language meant to mystify or deceive (700) (728) (1312)
635.	'I want to rid the world of **mumbo**-jumbo'	reputed last words of William Morris (19th c. pioneer of Design) (367)
636.	A **kangaroo** court	unjust or partial, ad hoc tribunal (80) (502) (1042)
637.	A kangaroo **Mouse**/Hare Kangaroo	small types of kangaroo (Aust.) (699)
638.	The Kangaroo **Paw**	the national flower of Australia (389)
639.	Kangaroo **petrol**/start	reference to inexpert vehicle clutch control (843) (1456)

640.	A Kangaroo **Rat**	a small kangaroo-like animal (699)
641.	The **leopard** cannot change his spots	one's basic nature stays the same (586) (750) (1502)
642.	To beard the **lion** in his den	to challenge someone powerful on his home ground (300) (362) (695)
643.	The Lion **City**	Singapore (derived from the Sanskrit word) (688) (747) (1131)
644.	Lions led by **donkeys**	reference to private soldiers and their Generals – 1st W. War (111) (1028) (1295)
645.	Lion-**hearted**	courageous; generous (147) (308) (1436)
646.	A lion **hunter**	a collector of celebrity acquaintances cf. *Pickwick Papers* – Dickens (584)
647.	To lion**ise** someone	to glorify him (687) (1022)
648.	To put one's head in the lion's **mouth**	to ask for trouble (627) (642) (695)
649.	To **paint** a lion from the claw	to draw a conclusion on almost no evidence (336) (572) (801)

650.	A lion in the **path**/way	a pretext for laziness or inaction (866) (1114)
651.	The lion's **share**	predominantly the greater part (origin: Aesop's fable, where the lion took all) (749) (1065)
652.	To be **thrown** to the lions	to be abandoned to a harsh fate (168) (709)
653.	To twist/pull the Lion's **tail**	to test the patience of the British people (95) (141)
654.	To **take** a lion for a walk	to make wild or unsupported statements (693) (813) (1216)
655.	**Lynx**-eyed	sharp-eyed (499) (516) (1534)
656.	A **Monkey**	£500 (sl.); $500 (US sl.); a sheep (Aust. sl.) (281)
657.	To monkey **around**	to fool about (248) (394) (527)
658.	As **artful**/clever as a wagonload of monkeys	very crafty or ingenious (541) (630) (1035)

659.	To have a monkey on one's **back**	to bear a grudge; to be high on drugs cf. to put a monkey on someone: to cast a spell on him; bring him bad luck (181) (212) (1388)
660.	As much fun as a **barrel-load** of monkeys	no fun at all (ironic) (261) (1361)
661.	A monkey-**bite**	a kiss that leaves a red mark (455) (1004)
662.	Cold enough to freeze the **balls** off a brass monkey	bitterly cold (naut.) – ships' cannon balls, stored in the 'monkey' contracted and fell through (31) (408) (1458)
663.	Monkey **business**	underhand or slightly dishonest activity (392) (1566) (1037)
664.	As mischievous/ **cheeky** as a monkey	lit.(70) (190)
665.	To **get** someone's monkey up	to anger him (715) (1317) (1444)
666.	Not to **give** a monkey's	not to care in the least (378) (1350)
667.	To **make** a monkey out of someone	to make a fool of him (196) (491)

668.	'I was addressing the **organ-grinder**, not the monkey'	rude remark made to someone who has just interrupted one (40) (926) (931)
669.	To pay with monkey **money**	to 'sweet'-talk one's way out of paying; to defraud (French) (392)
670.	Pay **peanuts** and you'll get monkeys	good quality has to be paid for (peanuts: a derisory amount) (777) (1562)
671.	To **play** monkey with someone	to play jokes on him (Anglo-Indian) (41) (732) (1444)
672.	A **powder** monkey	a boy who carried ammunition (naut.) so, a person taken advantage of (365) (662); a dynamite expert
673.	A Monkey **Puzzle**	a type of tree with complex, intertwined branches (79) (533) (1061)
674.	A monkey**shine**	a mischievous joke or prank (39) (470) (528)
675.	**Softly**, softly, catchee monkey	caution and discretion bring results (730) (1148) (1259)

676.	A monkey **suit**	man's formal evening wear cf. a monkey jacket: short, close-fitting jacket (573) (834)
677.	More **trouble** than a cartload of monkeys	lit. reference to something very hard to control (83) (1166)
678.	To be a monkey's **uncle**	to be astonished (319) (488) (1270)
679.	A monkeys' **wedding**	sunshine accompanied by rain (SA) (48) (722) (1116)
680.	A Monkey-**wrench**	tool for gripping with adjustable jaw (480) (1221)
681.	'An **orang-utan** trying to play the violin'	describing the average husband – Balzac (435) (1572)
682.	To smell like a **polecat**	lit. (865) (1360)
683.	To have a hide like a **rhinoceros**	to be completely insensitive (378) (1439)
684.	A **Stag**	Stock Exchange term (a seller of new shares for immediate profit) (293) (598)

685.	A **stag** party	a party for men only, usually preceding a wedding (307) (420)
686.	To **stoat** a torn garment	to 'invisibly' mend it (376) (618)
687.	A **Tiger**	a final loud cheer, eg. 'hoorah' after 'hip, hip' (647)
688.	**Asian** Tigers	technologically and economically strong South East Asian States (643) (1101)
689.	A Tiger**eye**	a yellow coloured gemstone (21) (901)
690.	'With his tiger's **heart** wrapped in a player's hide'	– Greene, describing Shakespeare (489) (575)
691.	'Better to have **lived** one day as a tiger than a thousand years as a sheep'	– Tibetan saying (138) (450)
692.	A **paper**-tiger	anything less powerful than it seems (Chinese) (163) (1487)

693.	'They're **riding** a tiger that may ultimately devour them'	warning to Haitian coup leaders – Secretary of State Albright (US) cf. he who rides a tiger is afraid to dismount (Chinese) (654) (1437)
694.	To **tell** a tiger by its stripes	to identify a thing by its obvious features (750) (1261) (1462)
695.	To have a tiger by the **tail**	to engage in a dangerous or provocative act cf. to hold a wolf by the ears (5) (642) (648)
696.	'The tigers of **wrath** are wiser than the horses of instruction'	– William Blake (481) (921) (1573)
697.	'Tig**gers** don't like honey'	*The House at Pooh Corner* (A.A. Milne) (591)
698.	A **Tigon**	offspring of a tiger and a lioness (904) (1457)
699.	On the **wallaby**	travel by foot (Aust.) (ironic) (172) (283) (1343)
700.	**Weasel** words	words calculated to deceive (term used by Pres. T Roosevelt) cf. to weasel one's way in: to insinuate oneself (273) (634) (1159)

701.	To cry **wolf** (once too often)	to raise the alarm unnecessarily (until people stop believing you) (273) (710)
702.	A Wolf **Cub**	A junior Scout cf. an Eagle Scout (273) (710)
703.	To wolf one's **food**	to eat voraciously (1311) (1476)
704.	A man who lives with wolves learns to **howl**	you become like the company you keep (116) (346)
705.	To **keep** the wolf from the door	to have just enough (food) to survive (229) (821) (1062)
706.	A **lone** wolf	one who prefers his own company (223) (1204) (1373)
707.	A wolf **note**	a badly sounded musical note especially on the violin and cello (297) (305) (1012)
708.	A wolf in **sheep's** clothing	a dangerous imposter, cf. 'A sheep in sheep's clothing' – Churchill on Attlee (223) (263) (770)
709.	To **throw** someone to the wolves	to abandon him in order to escape oneself (168) (652)

710.	To sell a wolf **ticket**	to lie, bluff or boast (US) (701) (763) (1540)
711.	A wolf-**whistle**	whistle to show appreciation of a woman (often lascivious) (11) (744) (1477)

Farm Animals

712.	To act the **goat**	to play the fool (193) (196) (657) ('The Goat' – nickname of Lloyd George)
713.	A goat**ee**	small pointed beard worn on chin (717) (737)
714.	A prudent man does not make the goat his **gardener**	lit. (nothing edible escapes a goat's notice) (627) (720)
715.	To **get** someone's goat	to annoy him (665) (1316) (1317)
716.	Like a **mountain** goat	very agile (10) (1003)
717.	If the beard were all, a goat might **preach**	intelligent looks are not necessarily conclusive (445) (713)
718.	A **scape**goat	an innocent victim sacrificed to save others (44) (241) (753)

719.	A Goat**sucker**	a Nightjar (species that makes no nest – called a 'flying toad' in France) (762)
720.	**Watch** the goat and the cabbage will look after itself	lit. preventative action avoids accidents (500) (714)
721.	To be on the **hog's** back	to be very successful (23) (894) (1442)
722.	**Ground**hog Day	February 2nd (weather-divining day in Atlanta and other States (US)) (679) (1072)
723.	A Hogs**head**	a large cask with capacity (on average) of 100 gallons (757) (1307) (1320)
724.	To live **high** off the hog	to live the good life (359) (1224) (1442)
725.	Like a hog on **ice**	completely independent, or self-reliant (US) (31) (601)
726.	A **road** hog	a selfish driver (1351) (1456) (1499)
727.	To be hog-**tied**	to be trussed up; helpless (201) (352) (1446)
728.	Hog**wash**	nonsense (231) (634) (1312) (a hog: brush for cleaning ships' bottoms)

729.	To go the **whole** hog	to indulge to the full (359)(1345)
730.	To handle with **kid** gloves	to treat very gently or kindly (675) (1259) (1273)
731.	A kid**hunter**	a school-attendance (truancy) officer (481) (1096) (1166)
732.	To kid **someone**	to fool or harmlessly deceive him (470) (510) (671)
733.	To kidnap **someone**	to snatch him against his will (1110) (1446)
734.	To bed with the **lamb** and up with the lark	recipe for a long, healthy life (355) (568) (809)
735.	The **sacrificial** lamb	lit. after religious ritual (290) (718)
736.	Like a lamb to the **slaughter**	lit. unresisting (290) (1566)
737.	**Mutton**-chop whiskers	bushy sideburns popular in the 19th c. (284) (713)
738.	As **dead** as mutton	dead beyond any doubt; old-fashioned (493) (804) (1182)

739.	Mutton **dressed** up as lamb	old object disguised as young – usually an older woman trying to look younger (351) (750) (1502)
740.	To **get** back to our muttons	to return to the subject under discussion (origin French) (427) (935)
741.	**Leg** of mutton sleeves	sleeves puffed out at top and fitted from elbow to wrist (790) (1318)
742.	To bleed/squeal like a stuck **pig**	to bleed profusely/squeal loudly (1179) (1381) (1536)
743.	Easier ways to kill a pig than drowning it in **butter**	advice to keep things simple (55) (1049)
744.	A male **chauvinist** pig	obnoxious, macho, sexist male (240) (279) (414)
745.	To make a pig's **ear** out of something	to make a mess of it (364) (825) (1359)
746.	'In a pig's **eye**!'	exclamation of disbelief (US) (242) (748)
747.	The pig/hog **farm**	the city of York (from the old English); so New York derives from 'the new pig farm' (643)

748.	'Pigs might **fly**!'	expression of disbelief (a pig-jump: a jump by horse from all four legs (Aust.) (sl.) (242) (303) (746)
749.	As **greedy** as a pig	lit. cf. as sick as a pig (508) (651) (1476)
750.	'What can you expect from a pig but a **grunt**?'	expect people to behave according to character (641) (739) (1502)
751.	**Happy** as a pig in clover/muck	in one's element (400) (401) (511)
752.	**Higgledy**-piggledy	in a complete mess or out of correct order (9) (105) (486)
753.	Pig in the **middle**	one who loses out or takes the blame (372) (718)
754.	To make a pig of **oneself**	to overeat, overindulge cf. to pig it (508) (749)
755.	He couldn't stop a pig in a **passage**	reference to a bow-legged person (subtly pej.) (551) (811)
756.	To buy a pig in a **poke**	to buy unseen; to take a risk (a poke: narrow basket with projecting front, hindering proper inspection) (19) (187) (1569)

757.	Pigs	dregs or sediment of wine etc. (723) (1307)
758.	To **sweat** like a pig	lit. (104) (1515)
759.	A pig**tail**	type of plaited hairstyle (284) (377) (971)
760.	Pig**gy**back	riding on someone's back (origin: pick-a-back) (1108)
761.	A pig**gy** bank	child's money box (originally in shape of a pig) (74) (857) (1544)
762.	A More**pork**	name for a nightjar in Australia (719); and an owl in New Zealand (541) (1351)
763.	To tell **porkies**	to tell lies (porkies: diminutive of 'pork pies' – rhyming slang) (710) (1540)
764.	To **ram** home	to force into place; to strongly express a point of view (228) (262)
765.	Stiff as a ram**rod**	very stiff or rigid (1295)
766.	A **water** ram	hydraulic device for raising river water (477) (800) (1050)

767.	**Sheep's** beard	low price, high nicotine content tobacco (S.E. Asia 2nd W. War) (442) (1468)
768.	The **black** sheep of the family	relative with a bad reputation; a disgrace to the family (718) (1296)
769.	To **count** sheep	to try to beat insomnia (169) (203) (274)
770.	'Like being savaged by a **dead** sheep'	Dennis Healey responding to Sir Geoffrey Howe's attack upon him. (pol.) (494) (613) (970)
771.	To make sheep's **eyes** at	to gaze adoringly at (loved one) (357) (478) (1183)
772.	To separate the sheep from the **goats**	to divide the best from the rest (26) (547)
773.	Sheep**ish**	bashful; self-effacing (77) (123)
774.	As well be hanged for a sheep as a **lamb**	if a small crime is harshly punished, you might as well commit a greater one (origin: former death penalty for sheep-stealing) (124) (645)

775.	To **lose** a sheep for a ha' porth of tar	a cheap and simple step may prevent a heavy loss (the word 'sheep' became corrupted to 'ship') (434)
776.	**Sow**belly	savoury 'nibbles' (US) cf. pork scratchings (UK.) (1188)
777.	You **can't** make a silk purse out of a sow's ear	advice to accept life's limitations (670) (1462)
778.	'I **compose** as a sow widdles'	effortlessly and profusely – Mozart (230) (544)
779.	'As a jewel of gold in a **swine's** snout'	'a fair woman without discretion' (Proverbs, Bible) (pej.) (813) (1516)
780.	To cast **pearls** before swine	to waste effort or resources on those who will not appreciate the gesture (210) (224) (384)
781.	Swine, **women** and bees are not for turning	reference to obstinacy (very pej.) (240) (279)
782.	A Bell**wether**	leading ram in flock – so a pioneer, adventurer (1330)

Other Animals

783.	The **Badger** Game	man lured by woman then blackmailed (a 'lure': device for recalling hawks) (204) (617) (1171)
784.	To **badger** someone	to keep on at him; to goad him cf. to bait: to tease and bully (182) (1419)
785.	A **Bat**	a prostitute (a Bathouse: a brothel) (US sl.) (942) (1131) (1347); brick broken at one end (1104)
786.	To have bats in the **belfry**	to be mad or eccentric cf. bats, batty (532) (812) (1527)
787.	**Blind** as a bat	lit. (though most species of bats are keensighted) (1150) (1454) (1569)
788.	To bat one's **eyes**	to wink them repeatedly (to bat: to flap wings of bird) (1279)

789.	Like a bat out of **hell**	extremely fast (52) (328) (1383)
790.	Batwing **sleeves**	loose, floppy sleeves, narrowing at the wrist (741) (1318)
791.	A **beaver**	lower part of helmet (602) (941); female genitalia (US sl.) (76) (583)
792.	To beaver **away**	to work hard (968) (1305) (1519)
793.	An **eager** beaver	very keen or willing worker (266) (269) (1382)
794.	To **buck** up one's ideas	to become more positive (1414) (1428)
795.	'If you try to buck the **market**, the market will buck you'	– Margaret Thatcher (1191) (1482)
796.	Buck-**toothed**	having teeth that protrude (551) (811)
797.	To buck the **trend**	to deviate from the rule; to break with fashion (312) (1356)
798.	A **bunny** hop	a light, accelerating jump in ice-skating (31) (127) (555)

799.	A snow **bunny**	female skier or learner (561) (1353)
800.	A **camel**	a device for raising sunken ships (766) (902) (1152)
801.	The camel's **nose**	insignificant pointer to a far greater problem. cf. the tip of the iceberg (802) (1016) (1560)
802.	The last **straw** breaks the camel's back	a small setback after several others can trigger off disaster (801)
803.	A **deers**talker	kind of cloth hat favoured by Sherlock Holmes (159) (182) (1241)
804.	Dead as a **dinosaur**	exceedingly dead (493) (738)
805.	'With Donne whose muse on **dromedary** trots, Wreathe iron pokers into true love knots'	reference to poetic 'conceits' for which John Donne was famous – S.T. Coleridge (911) (1471)
806.	A **guinea pig**	(person) used for experiment (718) (1439); old Stock Exchange term for a profiteer

807. 'First catch your **hare**'

part of recipe for hare pudding – Dr John Hill (alias Mrs Glasse) 18th c. (adapted) (336) (572) (1112)

808. **Chase** two hares and you'll catch neither

lit. if one divides one's energy and resources, nothing is accomplished (92) (225) (1352)

809. 'Whether my hare's **foot** or (my) pill of turpentine'

reflecting on the true reason for his continuing good health – Samuel Pepys (353) (734) (1081)

810. A Hare and **Hounds**

common term for a paper chase (518) (935) (1455)

811. A hare **lip**

a slightly split upper lip (551) (755) (796)

812. **Mad** as a March hare

completely unpredictable (415) (532) (786) cf. mad as a hatter: origin – irate as an adder

813. To **start** a hare

to open a fresh topic of conversation (1516); to generate a rumour (43) (654)

814. Don't make a shirt out of a **hedgehog** skin

do not deliberately act against your own interest (118) (620) (1537)

815.	**Lemming** behaviour	self-destructive; recklessly following others (444) (1330) (1331)
816.	A **mole**	a spy (3) (1538); a small pigmented area of skin (345); a machine for tunnelling (298); a jetty (267)
817.	To make a mountain out of a **mole**hill	to make a great fuss over a small matter (288) (1002) (1049)
818.	A **Mouse**	a small device to direct the cursor on a computer (987); a dark swelling, (black eye) (1128); retaining knot on rope (naut.) (851)
819.	**Behave** like a mouse and the cat will eat you	it is unwise to be too timid or to act out of character (193) (197)
820.	To **burn** the barn to get rid of the mice	to take measures out of all proportion to the problem (1002) (1049)
821.	As poor as a **church** mouse	the poorest of the poor (150) (565) (1487)
822.	A mous**er**	cat adept at catching mice (24) (440)

823.	'His **fingers** move like mice along the keyboard'	contemporary account of Schubert's piano playing (1372)
824.	The mouse with a single **hole** is soon caught	advice to diversify (913) (1245)
825.	A Mickey Mouse **job**	an unreliable or amateurish piece of work (364) (745)
826.	To **Mickey** Mouse	to match music with action of animated films (US) (245) (424) (477)
827.	As **quiet**/timid as a mouse	lit. (317) (341) (406)
828.	'Always leave **room** for the mouse'	instructions on mouse-trap box (434)
829.	The best laid **schemes** of mice and men often go astray	even the best thought-out plans can fail – Robert Burns (233)
830.	*The Mousetrap*	famous, long-running play by Agatha Christie (424) (1554)
831.	To see **white** mice	to see spots before your eyes (German) (612) (1567)

832.	A **Panda** Car	type of police car with blue and white markings, resembling panda (UK) (600) (1430)
833.	A **Panda** Crossing	type of pedestrian road crossing (UK) (286) (523)
834.	A **Penguin** suit	man's formal evening wear (black suit with tails worn with white shirt) (573) (1222) (1505)
835.	Prickly as a **porcupine**	very irritable and over-sensitive (304) (1429) (1568)
836.	To play **possum**	to simulate death (136) (1313)
837.	A **rabbit**	a poor games player – especially of golf and tennis (799) (1344)
838.	To rabbit an **area**	to 'clear' the rabbit population (547)
839.	To **breed** like rabbits	lit. (pej.) (285) (1363)
840.	Rabbit's **ears**	an indoor television aerial
841.	A rabbit's **foot**	a good luck charm (7) (213) (1390)

842.	To produce a rabbit from a **hat**	to improvise cleverly despite few resources (1452) (1473) (1550)
843.	A **jack**rabbit start	jerky departure in motor car through haste or inexperience of driver (639) (1456)
844.	To rabbit **on** about something	to talk non-stop (usually about trivial things) – origin: constant twitching movements of rabbit's mouth (205) (235) (1535)
845.	A rabbit **punch**/chop	a sharp blow using flat or side of the hand (1128)
846.	To tree the **racoon**	to trap or corner someone (861) (1506); to resolve a problem (337) (338)
847.	To be **rat-**arsed/tailed	to be completely inebriated (525) (945) (1309)
848.	Like rats **deserting** a sinking ship	abandoning others when disaster strikes (168) (1335) (1464)
849.	Like a **drowned** rat	wet to the skin (108) (902)
850.	A **frat** rat	a member of a university fraternity (93) (1054)

851.	Rat-**lines**	cords fixed across a ship's shrouds (masthead) to form a ladder (29) (486) (526)
852.	A rat's **nest**	an untidy, mess (486) (752)
853.	To rat on **someone**	to betray his confidence (1153) (1186) (1187)
854.	A **pack** rat	a hoarder of worthless trifles (534) (867)
855.	Coming out like **poisoned** rats	reference to late risers (from bed) (pej.) (a cow pillow: large cotton-filled pillow) (India) (203) (866)
856.	The rat **race**	the treadmill of modern society (160) (1379) (1380)
857.	A **rug** rat	a baby (570) (604) (1096)
858.	To **smell** a rat	to suspect foul play (263) (928)
859.	A rat-**tail** comb	a comb with long, thin handle (284) (759) (1150)
860.	A rat-**tail** hinge	a cupboard hinge with a vertical brace (1008)
861.	Like a rat in a **trap**	desperate and dangerous (846) (1283) (1506)
862.	A **Seal**point Ragdoll	a passive breed of cat (38) (866)

863.	A **Sealy**ham	a kind of terrier dog (154) (157)
864.	A **shrew**	a scolding woman (280) (883)
865.	As welcome as a **skunk**	wholly unwanted; unpopular (20) (179) (682)
866.	To be **sloth**ful	to be lazy or inert (650) (1114)
867.	A **squirrel**	a compulsive hoarder; slightly eccentric person (534) (854)
868.	To **squirrel** out of something	to wriggle out of a duty etc. (983) (1108)

Fish & Crustaceans

869.	A **barnacle** goose	species of Arctic wild goose (a barnacle: unwelcome social hanger-on) (1341)
870.	To **carp** about something	to complain constantly (280) (287) (509)
871.	**Carp** love	romance between elderly people (1524)
872.	Happy as a **clam** at high water	very cheerful (166) (511) (1011)
873.	**Clammy**	unpleasantly damp or sticky (898)
874.	To clam **up**	to become (and stay) silent (1395) (1523)
875.	To **cockle**	to wrinkle or pucker (22) (484)
876.	A cockle**shell**	a small, light boat (885) (1029) (1152)

877.	Enough to **warm** the cockles of your heart	giving a glowing, kindly feeling (cockles being heart-shaped) (412) (1556)
878.	'The home of the bean and the **cod**'	description of Boston – J.C. Bossidy (747)
879.	A **Cape** Cod Lighter	porous, paraffin-soaked stone with handle, for lighting fire (US) (114) (990)
880.	'My music has a taste of cod**fish** in it'	– Edvard Grieg
881.	A cod**piece**	bag covering genitals to emphasise virility – Europe: 16th c. & 17th c. (1034) (1143) (1377) cf. a codling: variety of apple
882.	Cods**wallop**	nonsense (231) (302) (367)
883.	A **crab**	an irritable person (864) (883) (960); a wild sour apple (881)
884.	To crab an **aircraft**	to aim it sideways on into a cross-wind (366) (1012) (1507)
885.	To **catch** a crab	to make a faulty stroke in rowing boat (876) (1263) (1458)

886.	A crabbed **hand**	hard to read handwriting (too close together) (1078)
887.	Crab**s**	pubic lice (581) (1432)
888.	To crab **someone**	violently abuse him verbally (564) (1014) (1220)
889.	To **throw** crabs	to throw a pair of aces at dice (1136) (1140)
890.	A **dab** hand	a handy person; a craftsman (69) (dab: small, edible flatfish)
891.	A **Dolphin**	buoy or mooring for boats (876) (1029); symbol of social love in medieval art
892.	A **dolphin** kick	a quick kicking action while swimming (1000) (1232)
893.	As slippery as an **eel**	lit. (pej.) cf. to wriggle like an eel ('Eel': nickname for New Englander) (US)
894.	All's **fish** that comes to his/the net	reference to some thing or someone that is unfailingly successful (721) (913)
895.	'Fish, or cut **bait**'	'do something or go away' (524) (1212) (1489)

896.	A **big** fish in a small pond	an important person in a small community (23) (1292)
897.	To fish for **compliments**	to seek flattering comments by guiding the conversation (132) (1147)
898.	As **cold** as a dead fish	unresponsive or unfriendly (873) (914)
899.	To **drink** like a fish	to drink a lot of alcohol (278) (1024) (1567)
900.	To go on a fishing **expedition**	to ask unfair or unfounded questions in the hope of gleaning information (962) (1162) (1525)
901.	A Fish-**eye**	a type of photographic lens (1080) ; a dull-looking gemstone (689); blotchy plasterwork (512)
902.	To **feed** the fishes	to drown (800) (1152) (1418)
903.	A fish **fight**	a fight between women (25)
904.	Neither fish, **flesh** nor good red herring	an indefinable or hybrid thing, impossible to categorise (174) (698) (909)

905.	'There was always something fishy about the **French**'	– Noel Coward (pej.) (141) (1105)
906.	Like living in a **gold**-fish bowl	lacking privacy; exposed (59)
907.	After three days, fish and **guests** begin to stink	lit. (very pej.) (179) (865) (1453)
908.	A **half**-warmed fish	classic 'Spoonerism' for 'a half-formed wish' (1163) (1534)
909.	A different **kettle** of fish	reference to something not at all similar (originally 'kiddle': a fish trap made of basketwork) (221) (256) (904)
910.	A pretty **kettle** of fish	a fine mess or muddle; an embarrassing situation (752) (939)
911.	'You... make **little** fishes talk... like whales'	complimenting Dr Johnson on his wonderful prose style – Oliver Goldsmith (805) (993) (1413)
912.	'A **motherless** son is a fish in low water'	– Burmese saying (419) (1203)

913.	Plenty **more** fish in the sea	many other available options – usually said of romantic affairs (894) (945)
914.	As **mute** as a fish	completely silent (62) (827) (1189)
915.	An **odd** fish	an eccentric or bizarre person (576) (1023) (1298)
916.	To fish something **out**	to unearth a hidden or missing object (900) (948) (1277)
917.	'I have my **own** fish to fry'	'I have my own preoccupations' – Cervantes (113) (553) (1271)
918.	To cry '**stinking** fish'	to condemn one's own products, actions, or friends (19) (139) (1464)
919.	To **swim** like a fish	lit. (400) (1109)
920.	A fish**tail**	rear end swerve of vehicle (1456) (1499)
921.	'It is better to **teach** a man to fish than to give him a fish'	– Mao Tse Tung (696)
922.	A **tin** fish	a torpedo (937) (989); a type of coin (497)

923.	To stick out like a fish in a **tree**	to look completely out of place (475) (925) (928)
924.	To fish in **troubled** waters	to profit from other people's misfortune or misery (160) (934) (1271)
925.	Like a fish out of **water**	completely out of one's element (475) (923) cf. to flounder: to struggle and plunge; (flounder: a flat fish)
926.	A slap in the face with a **wet** fish	a gross insult or rebuff (668) (931) (1528)
927.	To **swear** like a fishwife	to swear expertly (433) (1220)
928.	Fish**y**	suspicious, noticeably wrong (858) (923)
929.	A **fluke**	an unexpected piece of good luck (7); the triangular point of an anchor (fluke: a flat fish) (1152)
930.	**Flukes**	the lobes making up a whale's tail (961); a series of chance breezes (44) (944)
931.	A poke in the eye with a wet **haddock**	an undeserved remark or incident (668) (926)

932.	**Herring**bone	a pattern in fabrics, brickwork or wooden floors etc. (183) (785)
933.	As **dead** as a herring	lit. (reference to strong smell when dead) (493) (738) (804)
934.	The Herring **Pond**	the Atlantic fishing grounds (924)
935.	A **red** herring	a false clue often laid deliberately to mislead; an irrelevant diversion (518) (810) (1174)
936.	About as far through as a **kipper**	very thin (kipper: a smoked herring) (550) (1069) (1088) cf. as skinny as a cuckoo (French)
937.	To cling like a **limpet**	to hold on very tight (so, a limpet mine: adhesive ship mine) (182) (922)
938.	A **Lobster** Back	18th c. British soldier in red-coated uniform (US) (289) (436)
939.	To **blush** like a lobster	facial reddening, as a sign of embarrassment (910)
940.	A lobster **pot**	a child's play-pen (US) (188) (604) (857)

941	A lobster-**tail** helmet	a type of cavalry helmet worn in English Civil War – 17th c. (602) (791)
942.	A **mackerel**	a pimp (procurer of prostitutes) (785) (1131)
943.	'**Holy** mackerel!'	interjection of wonderment (319) (488)
944.	A mackerel **sky**	a blotchy sky, reminiscent of a mackerel's body (267) (276) (679) cf. a mackerel breeze: a strong breeze, ideal for mackerel fishing
945.	Pickled (pissed) as a **newt**	completely inebriated (sl.) (847) (1085) (1309)
946.	A Prairie **Oyster**	a cocktail drink (Canada) (146) (278) (374)
947.	The world's your **oyster**	reference to life's many opportunities (412) (611) (1492)
948.	'He who would search for **pearls** must dive below'	the best things often lie hidden – Dryden (571) (577) (916)
949.	The **Pearly** Gates	Heaven's door; teeth (sl.) (1556)

950.	A turn**pike**	a toll-gate (605) (949) (a pike: diving position with body bent double – named after the fish)
951.	Packed as tightly as **sardines**	lit. – sardines are vacuum-packed (59) (1230)
952.	**Shark**-repellent	an action that prevents a corporate take-over (615)
953.	'But a **shrimp** of an author'	self-description – Thomas Gray (197) (1022)
954.	A **silverfish**	a silvery, wingless insect fond of damp places (227)
955.	To **spawn** something	to create: give birth to (570) (1324)
956.	To **sponge** off someone	to live off them; to cadge (976) (1190)
957.	Sponge**rs**	people sent in deliberately to nuclear installations to absorb ambient radioactivity (1176)
958.	To **throw** in the sponge	to concede defeat (37) (173)
959.	A **sprat** to catch a mackerel	a small outlay calculated to secure big profits (204) (617) (1033)

960. An old **trout**   a crotchety old woman (81)
                                     (883) (1099)

961. To have a **whale** of   to enjoy oneself immensely
     a time   (930) (1513)

962. To **winkle** out   to discover by tenacity (900)
                                     (1113) (1162)

963. **Winkle**pickers   shoes with very pointed
                                     toes (277) (982) (1558)

Insects & Spiders

964.	To have **ants** in one's pants	to be fidgety or agitated (8) (49) (73)
965.	A **Bee**	a meeting or club that combines business with pleasure (US) (69) (313) (1478)
966.	To have a bee in one's **bonnet**	to be troubled or obsessed by something (236) (964) (995)
967.	'As **brisk** as a bee in conversation'	his description of Tom Birch – Dr Johnson (205)
968.	**Busy** as a bee	constantly back and forth (792) (1027) (1417)
969.	A Beehive **Clock**	a Connecticut shelf clock (also called a Flatiron Clock because of its shape) – mid 19th c. (1368)

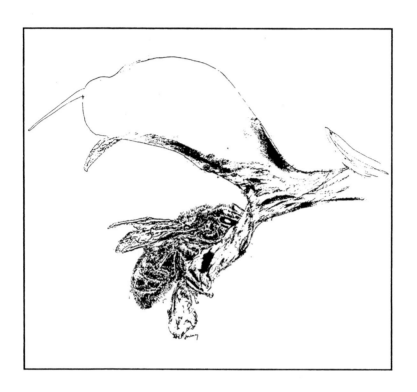

970.	To be bitten by a **dead** bee	to be attacked by something previously thought harmless (memorably used in 'To Have And Have Not' – Bogart film) (770) (1164) (1482)
971.	A Bee**hive**	lady's hairstyle with hair bunched into high 'bun' (284) (377) (759)
972.	Bees and **honey**	money – UK rhyming slang (90) (281) (1050)
973.	The bee's **knees**	the best (47) (66) (1562)
974.	To make a bee**line**	to go directly and quickly (255) (485)
975.	Like bees around the honey-**pot**	attracted in large numbers (1060) (1424) (1491)
976.	To **put** the bee on someone	to cadge or borrow money (originally the 'b' of 'bee' stood for 'bite') (US) (956) (1190)
977.	Bee**stings**	first milk after giving birth (used especially of cows) (16) (955)
978.	Bee**swing**	second crust in old wine or old port (1307)

979.	A **Beetle**	large pestle for mashing potatoes (Irish) (983)
980.	To beetle **along**	to hurry along, heedless of other people (968) (1027) (1417)
981.	To be beetle**browed**	to frown in concentration or anger; to have a pronounced forehead (as did Debussy)
982.	Beetle**crushers**	large and heavy boots (417) (963)
983.	To **dodge** the beetle	to avoid responsibility; to shirk a job (Irish) (391) (979) (1108)
984.	A **bug**	a weight allowance for junior jockeys (201) (1462); a kind of tiepin (1001) (1107)
985.	To be **bitten** by a bug	to be enthusiastic (588) (1208)
986.	To **catch** a bug	to suffer a minor illness (345) (998)
987.	A **computer** bug	an error in a computer programme (818) (1403)

988.	To **de**bug	to clear up a computer error; to 'demystify' a subject (818) (1403) cf. the Millennium Bug.
989.	A **doodle**bug	a flying bomb – especially German bombs in 2nd W. War (365) (624) (1176)
990.	A **fire**bug	an arsonist (114) (879)
991.	A **jitter**bug	a very nervous person (the Jitterbug: type of jazz dance) (1) (629) (1000)
992.	A **Kissing** bug / Barber bug	an insect whose faeces cause Chagas' disease (fever/heart-inflammation) (S. America) (998) (1059)
993.	'The difference between **lightning** and a lightning bug'	contrasting a word that 'fits' with one that does not – Mark Twain (lightning bug: a firefly) (911) (1413)
994.	A **litter**bug	a deliberate litter-dropper (1040) (1044)
995.	To have something bugging **one**	to be troubled by something (966) (1427) cf. a bugbear: an irritant
996.	To bug a **room**	to listen secretly by means of an electronic device (1013) (1046)

997.	As **snug** as a bug in a rug	cosily ensconced – used on the death of a child's pet squirrel by Benjamin Franklin (552) (607)
998.	A **Super**bug	a bacterium that is resistant to antibiotics (986)
999.	To **bumble** about	to move clumsily or aimlessly (295) (340)
1000.	The **Butterfly**	a fast swimming stroke (892) (1232); a modern dance (629) (991)
1001.	A Butterfly **Bow**	a type of formal necktie (984) (1093) cf. a batswing bow
1002.	'Who **breaks** a butterfly upon a wheel?'	a reference to overdoing things – Alexander Pope (817) (820) (1049)
1003.	'**Float** like a butterfly and sting like a bee'	– 'Mohammed Ali' (heavyweight boxer) (335) (1003) (1047)
1004.	A butterfly **kiss**	brushing one's eyelash against another person's cheek (189) (661) (1421)
1005.	A butterfly **knife**	a clasp knife with handles that close on either side of the blade

1006.	A butterfly **screw**	a screw with finger grips (1090) (1154) (1552)
1007.	Butterflies in the **stomach**	nervousness or stage fright (73) (1554) (1559)
1008.	A butterfly **table**	a table with leaves able to fold up or down (860) (1401) cf. a butterfly roof: roof in form of an 'M'
1009.	A **Caterpillar** (trademark)	a heavy vehicle using all-terrain tracks (298) (477) (766)
1010.	The **Caterpillar**	fairground machine that articulates like the insect (1302)
1011.	As chirpy as a **cricket**	always lively and good-humoured (511) (872) (1200)
1012.	A **drone**	a constant ground-note in music (eg. bagpipes) (707) (1115); a pilot – less aircraft. (366) (884) cf. to drone on
1013.	To **earwig**	to try to influence by insinuation (216); to eavesdrop (rarer) (996) (1046)

1014	To **give** someone an earwigging / a wigging	to reprimand or scold him (888) (1220)
1015.	Like a **throttled** earwig	frantic; hyperactive (8) (1027) (1184)
1016.	A mere **flea**-bite	a tiny inconvenience (said by Disraeli of the National Debt) (437) 1066) (1074)
1017.	Flea-**bitten** / ridden	in very poor condition (1069) (1340)
1018.	'Just once I'd like to be a flea instead of a **dog**'	referring to the US's super power status – Pres. Bill Clinton (after Mark Twain) (1195)
1019.	To get a flea in one's **ear**	to be admonished (1084) (1465); to be dropped a hint (216)
1020.	To feel as **fit** as a flea	to be in bouncing good health (97) (264)
1021.	A flea **market**	a street market for second-hand goods (1017) (1069)
1022.	'I do honour the **very** flea of his dog'	– Francis Bacon 17th c. (647) (953)
1023.	A **fly** in amber	a curiosity; an anachronism (915) (1298)

1024.	A **bar**fly	a heavy drinker (899) (1234) (1567)
1025.	A fly**blow**	illegitimate person (very pej.) (491) (839)
1026.	Fly-**blown** / specked	covered in dirty marks (625) (1057)
1027.	Like a **blue** arsed fly	in a great hurry (968) (980) (1417)
1028.	To **drop** like flies	to die in large numbers (644) (1295)
1029.	A **fire**fly	a small sailing dinghy; an insect with phosphorescent glow cf. a glow-worm (876) (891) (1458)
1030.	A **gad**fly	a tiresome, overdemanding person (715) (784) (1419)
1031.	A fly-**half**	a position on the Rugby field cf. a wing (three quarter) (201)
1032.	A fly **leaf**	opening page of book containing title, author's name etc. (109) (1039) (1441)
1033.	To **lose** a fly to catch a trout	to risk a little in order to gain a lot (204) (959)

1034.	A (**man's**) fly/flies	a zip giving access to the crotch in trousers (881) (1143)
1035.	'No flies on **me**'	astute; not easily deceived (too alert even for the flies to land) (621) (630) (658)
1036.	'A closed **mouth** catches no flies'	slander can come back to haunt one – Cervantes (43) (1186) (1485)
1037.	A fly-by-**night**	a shady or crooked 'operator' (134) (462) (1195)
1038.	A fly in the **ointment**	a minor defect spoiling the whole (1064) (1247)
1039.	A fly **paper**	a pamphlet; a sticky fly trap (1032) (1045)
1040.	Fly-**posting**	the unauthorised fixing of posters (994) (1044)
1041.	A fly **sheet**	the outer part of a tent (167) (238)
1042.	'Where the **small** flies were caught and the great brake through'	comparing bad legislation with cobwebs – Bacon (2) (80) (636)

1043.	**Spanish** fly	an aphrodisiac; a member of the beetle family (455) (1358) (1363)
1044.	Fly-**tipping**	the unauthorised dumping of rubbish (994) (1040)
1045.	A **Venus** Fly-Trap	species of plant that consumes flies (1036) (1039)
1046.	To be a fly on the **wall**	to listen in invisibly to other people's private conversations (3) (996) (1013)
1047.	A Fly**weight**	a lightweight boxer (approx. 48 to 51 kg) (335) (1003) (1275)
1048.	A fly **wheel**	a heavy wheel on a machine (202) (766) (1129)
1049.	To strain at a **gnat** and swallow a camel	to confuse the relative importance of things (817) (820) (1002)
1050.	A **grasshopper**	a shopper (rhyming slang) (90) (972); an oil derrick (477) (766)
1051.	**Knee-high** to a grasshopper	short of stature; very young (188) (382) (1196)

1052.	Grasshopper-**minded**	having a short attention span; mercurial cf. butterfly-minded (375)
1053.	**Grub**	food (sl.) (1188) (1452)
1054.	A **grade**-grubber	a hardworking student (pej. US) (850)
1055.	To have the **mulli**grubs	to be in low spirits (88) (1364) (1422)
1056.	To grub**stake** someone	to provide him with venture capital (US) (131) (315) (323)
1057.	Grubb**y**/lousy	dirty (529) (625) (1026)
1058.	To bring a **hornets**' nest about one's ears	to create trouble; cf. to stir up a hornets' nest (1156) (1362)
1059.	To feel **jiggered**	to feel worn out or exhausted (a jigger: a parasitic insect – Africa) (992) (1374) (1385)
1060.	To swarm like **locusts**	to cluster round greedily, in great numbers (975) (1491)
1061.	A Locust **Tree**	a false Acacia (79) (533) (673)

1062	The locust **years**	times of intense poverty and need (used by Churchill) (705) (821)
1063.	To skin a **louse** for its hide	to be very mean (140) (398)
1064.	To louse something **up**	to spoil something; to get it completely wrong (US sl.) (745) (1038)
1065.	To be lousy **with**	to have too much of something (sl.) (651)
1066.	A **mite** bigger / smaller	a tiny fraction bigger / smaller (1016)
1067.	To **moth**ball something	to place it in protective storage pending further need (1226)
1068.	A **behe**moth	something of immense size or power (633) (1387)
1069.	Moth-**eaten**	lit. in a very poor state (1017) (1021) (1340)
1070.	A moth-**eaten** idea	an outmoded idea, that is not fundamentally sound (358) (1298)
1071.	To be drawn like a moth to a **flame**	to be irresistibly attracted cf. like flies to dung (751) (975) (1060)

1072.	A **Nit**	a unit of luminescence, eg. to measure quality of daylight (722) (1127); a silly person (1225)
1073.	The nitty **gritty**	the essential points (427)
1074.	To nit-**pick**	to quibble over minor details (437)
1075.	A **Roach**	home-made filter of marijuana cigarette (sl.) (110) (519)
1076.	A **Spider**	a motoring tool (282); a cueing rest in game of Snooker (1082)
1077.	'If you wish to live and thrive, let the spider run **alive**'	an old saying (841) (1081) (1390)
1078.	Spidery **handwriting**	lit. (886)
1079.	A spider-**hole**	a trench that conceals a sniper (564) (624)
1080.	A spider-**line**	a line in telescope for gauging exact position (162) (1574)
1081.	A **money** spider	a small spider reputed to bring prosperity (809) (1077) (1390)

1082.	A **Swan**-necked Spider	a projecting cueing rest in game of Snooker (1076)
1083.	A **Stick-Insect**	an insect that mimics a twig for camouflage (223) (1094)
1084.	To **tick** someone off	to admonish him (1019) (1220); to eliminate him (559) (1108)
1085.	Tight as a **tick**	extremely drunk (847) (945) (1309)
1086.	W.A.S.P.	a White Anglo Saxon Protestant (US) (191)
1087.	Wasp**ish**	irritable (603) (1274) (1317)
1088.	Wasp-**waisted**	having a very narrow waist (551) (628) (936)

Reptiles Etc.

1089. 'Oh conscience, what an **adder** art thou'

from *Christmas Stories* – Charles Dickens (1427)

1090. An **alligator** clip

an electrical clip resembling an alligator's snout (1006) (1552)

1091. 'Get across the river before you insult the mother **alligator**'

Haitian proverb (33) (51) (593)

1092. 'Symphonic **boa-constrictors**'

describing the Symphonies of Bruckner – Johannes Brahms (1315) (1528)

1093. A feather **boa**

lady's throat-wrap in form of a snake, 19th c. (423) (1001)

1094. A **chameleon**

person who changes allegiance too easily; a turncoat (from the lizard that blends in with its decor) (260) (375) (1083)

1095.	A **Copperhead**	a treacherous person (after a type of poisonous snake) (US) (84) (1137) (1142)
1096.	A **crocodile**	a line of children walking two by two (in France they often clutch a knotted rope) (188) (731) (857)
1097.	The **Crocodile**	Cuba (because of its shape) (614)
1098.	Crocodile **tears**	a pretence of sorrow, prior to a treacherous act (1095) (1137) (1393)
1099.	A **dragon**	a loud, tyrannical woman (81) (631) (883)
1100.	'An **habitation** for dragons and a court for owls'	– Song of Solomon
1101.	Dragon **Ladies**	women who wield great power and influence (S.E. Asia) (23) (688)
1102.	**Snap**dragon	a Christmas game (snatching raisins from a dish of burning brandy) (15) (344)
1103.	To sow the dragon's **teeth**	to (innocently) sow the seeds of future discord (3) (46) (1165)

1104.	A **frog**	a Frenchman (sl. pej.) (905); part of a violin bow (387); hollow part of a house brick (785); part of a horse's sole (1439)
1105.	Frog-**bashing**	strong criticism of the French (pej.) (905)
1106.	Frogs' **eggs**	tapioca pudding (161) (1146)
1107.	A frog **fastener**	spindle-shaped device for fastening coats etc. – so a 'frogged coat/jacket' (206) (984)
1108.	To **leap**frog	to improve one's ranking by jumping over those ahead (391) (983); a children's game (15) (760)
1109.	A frog**man**	an expert underwater swimmer (902) (919)
1110.	To frog**march**	to march a person between two others. (Originally to carry prisoner by arms and legs, facedown) (503) (733)
1111.	A frog in one's **throat**	hoarseness; cf. 'a cat in one's throat' (French) (185) (1236)

1112.	'Thus use your frog...'	from *The Compleat Angler* – Izaak Walton (336) (572) (807) cf. 'Oh, to be a frog and live aloof from care' – Theocritus
1113.	To **leech** something out	to suck or draw out. (Leeches are again playing an important role in medical science) (962) (1162)
1114.	To be a lounge **lizard**	to idle one's time away in fashionable circles cf. 'to lizard' (French) (522) (650) (866)
1115.	'Like trying to blow an **octopus**'	on playing the bagpipes – James Galway (Irish Flute player) (250) (305) (1012)
1116.	'That **dear** octopus from whose tentacles we never quite escape'	on the family – Dodie Smith (418) (679)
1117.	Like getting an octopus into a **matchbox**	classic definition of the word 'difficult' (1256)
1118.	A **reptile**	term of contempt, but also, on occasion, of endearment (84)

1119.	The **Reptile** Press	alternative for the term 'the gutter press' (pej.) (1032) ('I love the Press. It's what separates us from the animals' – Sylvester Stallone)
1120.	A **Salamander**	a workman's stove or heater for outside use (662)
1121.	A **Serpent**	an ancient, coiled musical instrument, much appreciated by woodworm (387) (1466) (1560)
1122.	'It **biteth** like a serpent and stingeth like an adder'	on alcoholic drink – 'Proverbs' Bible (1126) (1133)
1123.	A **civil** serpent	a civil servant (US) (1042) (1169) (1545)
1124.	The Serpent**ine**	a winding lake in Hyde Park London (133) (580)
1125.	A **slug**	a bullet (US) (93) (201) (1394)
1126.	To **have** a slug	to take a strong drink (US sl.) (1122) (1133)
1127.	A **Metric** Slug	a unit of mass in the metric system (1072)

1128.	To slug **someone**	to hit him hard (sl.) (564) (818) (845)
1129.	A **snail** cam	a part in a machine (1048) (1158)
1130.	At a **snail's** pace	scarcely mobile (237) (320) (1232) (snail mail: ordinary post pej.)
1131.	A **Snake**	the Police name for an officer posing as client in a brothel (Hong Kong/Singapore) (263) (643) (785); a device to clear blocked drains (1181) (1521)
1132.	'Lower than a snake's **belly**'	beneath contempt (84) (140)
1133.	Snake**bite**	strong alcoholic liquor (US) (1122) (1126)
1134.	Snake**bitten**	overwhelmed by many problems (340) (1385) (1511)
1135.	A **Black**snake	a person advocating abolition of slavery (US pej.) (77)
1136.	Snake's **eyes**	a pair of 'ones' in game of dice (889)

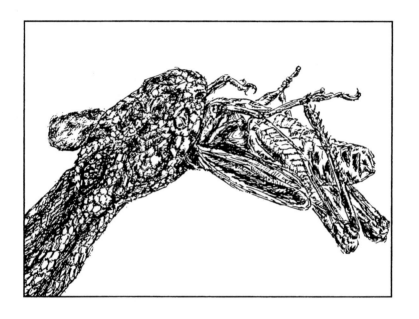

1137.	A snake in the **grass**	a treacherous enemy who pretends to be a friend (84) (1095) (1098)
1138.	Like a snake through **grass**	negotiating obstacles with ease (893)
1139.	Snake**heads**	syndicates that smuggle illegal immigrants (S.E. Asia) (159)
1140.	Snakes and **Ladders**	classic children's board game (15) (413) (560)
1141.	The Great **Rainbow** Snake	creator of the Human spirit (Native Australian)
1142.	Snake**stone**	a reputed cure for snake bites (1095) (1480) (1483)
1143.	The one-eyed **trouser** snake	a crude reference to the male organ (881) (1034)
1144.	A **Tadpole** Galaxy	a type of radio galaxy in the shape of a tadpole (65)
1145.	To eat another person's **toads**	to flatter him or do his 'dirty work' (132) (483) (1319)
1146.	Toad-in-the-hole	sausages cooked in batter (161) (1106) (1479)

1147.	To toady **up** to someone	to fawn on him. (132) (897) (1319) (A tody: a kind of kingfisher)
1148.	'The **tortoise** will usually beat the hare'	advocating patience in politics – John Major (613) (675)
1149.	'We **called** him Tortoise because he taught us'	*Alice in Wonderland* – Lewis Carroll (4) (27)
1150.	Tortoise**shell**	a yellowy-brown translucent material used to make combs and spectacles (787) (859); a butterfly (573) (606)
1151.	A **turtle**neck	a type of sweater with close fitting neck
1152.	To turn **turtle**	to capsize (385) (876) (1182)
1153.	To nourish a **viper** in one's bosom	to be let down or attacked by one whom one has helped (853) (1137) (1187)
1154.	A **Worm**	the spiral part of a screw (1006) (1131) (1158)
1155.	To be a **book**worm	to be an avid reader (109) (1032) (1441)

1156.	To open up a **can** of worms	to interfere unwisely and to one's cost (17) (158) (1058)
1157.	To **cheat** the worms	narrowly to survive a grave illness (902) (1160) cf. to feed the worms: to be dead
1158.	A worm **gear**	a gear in the form of a thread (1048) (1129)
1159.	To worm one's way **in**	to insinuate oneself; to enter by guile (700) (1147)
1160.	'The **Invisible** Worm'	Death – William Blake (246)
1161.	'**Man** cannot make a worm, yet he makes gods by the dozens'	– Montaigne
1162.	To worm something **out** of someone	to extract an object or information by patient and devious means (619) (962) (1113)
1163.	'Sir, you have **tasted** two whole worms'	addressing an undergraduate who had 'wasted two whole terms' – Rev. W.A. Spooner (attrib) (908) (1534)
1164.	Even a worm will **turn**	a warning similar to: 'beware the fury of a patient man' (103) (970)
1165.	Gall and worm**wood**	the source of (future) bitterness (1103) (1198)

General Terms

1166. 'Of all the **animals**, the boy is the most unmanageable'

– Plato (481) (677) (731)

1167. 'Men love women, women love **children** and children love animals'

a saying to explain the trouble with the world (338)

1168. 'The man as can form a' ackerate **judgment** of a' animal can form a' ackerate judgment of anything'

Pickwick Papers – Charles Dickens (195) (1293)

1169. 'Man is by nature a **political** animal'

– Aristotle (1123) (1425) (1545)

1170. 'A **two**-legged animal without feathers'

Man – Plato (476) (520)

1171.	Jail-**bait**	reference to an under-age seductress (US) (72) (783)
1172.	To rise to the **bait**	to react as intended (617) (959) (1231)
1173.	A **Bark**er	a 'crier' at a theatre, market stall or other public place (1475)
1174.	To bark **up** the wrong tree	to have the wrong idea (272) (909) (935)
1175.	To have a bark **worse** than one's bite	to be kinder than one seems (86) (98)
1176.	A **Barn**	the code-word to describe the probability/target area of certain nuclear reactions (957) (989)
1177.	To be **born** in a barn	someone always leaving the door open because he does not know any better (257)
1178.	Incapable of hitting the **side** of a barn	a very poor marksman (299) (534)
1179.	To **bay** for someone's blood	to seek his downfall (742) (1381) (1536)

1180.	To **bay** at the moon	to waste one's energy (99) (225) (418) (the Hunter's Moon: start of hunting season)
1181.	A **Beak**	a judge or magistrate (sl.) (596) (1261); a device to divert water from a roof (1131) (1521) (A parrot's beak: bony growth on spine-French)
1182.	To turn **belly** up	to die or fail (origin: action of dead fish in water) (738) (1152) cf. dead in the water: hopeless; beyond reprieve
1183.	To **bill** and coo	to behave as lovers (771) (1421) (1524)
1184.	To champ at the **bit**	to be very impatient (255) (1382) (1423) cf. to kick at the traces; to bridle (similar terms)
1185.	To take the **bit** between your teeth	to be resolute (5) (95) (269)
1186.	To back**bite**	to slander or speak ill of an absent person (43) (853) (1036)
1187.	To bite the **hand** that feeds you	to be stupidly ungrateful (409) (853) (1153)

1188.	To **have** a bite	to eat a snack (perhaps consisting of a Pikelet: a crumpet) (85) (1053) (1452)
1189.	'**Nobody's** going to bite you'	form of encouragement to a timid person to speak up or come forward (62) (75) (914)
1190.	To **put** the bite on someone	to borrow money from him (956) (976) (1460)
1191.	The biter bit	reference to the bully meeting his match (348) (795) (1482)
1192.	A hard-**bitten** person	a rough individual who has experienced hardship in life (176) (521) (631)
1193.	Once **bitten**, twice shy	learning by one's mistakes (51) (970)
1194.	To be **blinkered**	to have a narrow viewpoint (217) (1332) (1563)
1195.	A **bloodsucker**	an extortionist or sponger (pej.) (783) (1018) (1113)
1196.	To **blubber**	to weep like a child (188) (1051)

1197.	What's bred in the **bone** comes out in the flesh	a person's innate character will always emerge (586) (641) (750)
1198.	A bone of **contention**	a quibble likely to lead to major discord (1103) (1165)
1199.	To have a bone to **pick**	to have a minor difference of opinion (262) (1074) (A Merrythought: wishbone of a bird)
1200	**Bright-eyed** and bushy-tailed	alert and in fine form (97) (1011) (1428)
1201	To **bristle** with anger	to be furious (301) (422) (1274)
1202.	To **brood** over something	to sulk or allow something to rankle (75) (1420) (1422)
1203.	To be **broody**	to experience or display maternal (or paternal) feelings (404) (419) (912)
1204.	A **browser**	a person who chooses to avoid deep relationships with others (slightly pej.) (706)
1205.	**Brute** force and ignorance	the aggressive approach, devoid of sensitivity and subtlety (512) (631) (1570)

1206.	'Nasty, **brutish** and short'	a pessimistic view of human life – Hobbes (160) (1573)
1207.	To **butt** in	to interrupt rudely; cf. to ask someone to 'butt out': 'go away' (301) (1354) (1423)
1208.	To get a **buzz** out of something	to be excited by it or to enjoy it (588) (985)
1209.	A **buzz** saw	a circular saw (442) (496) (1400)
1210.	A buzz**er**	an electric bell with its hammer and gong removed (431); a wood-planing machine (NZ.) (546) (1209)
1211.	A buzz-**word**	a topical, contemporary saying
1212.	To cut the **cackle**	to stop talking and start acting (895) (1520)
1213.	To live in a gilded **cage**	to live as a prisoner, but in luxury (453)
1214.	To **rattle** someone's cage	to try and provoke a reaction from him (495) (1362)

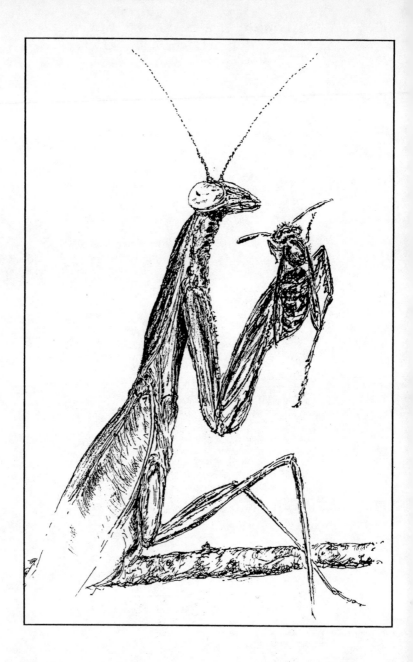

1215.	To be cagey	to be hesitant and non-committal (33) (675) (1259)
1216.	A **canard**	an unfounded rumour (654) (813)
1217.	To be **chirpy**	to be cheerful; have a positive outlook (1200) (1428)
1218.	The dawn **chorus**	birdsong at daybreak (355) (530) (568)
1219.	It's a **cinch**	saying to denote something is certain or very easy (249) (373) (1546) (a cinch: saddle-strap on horse)
1220.	To clapper**claw**	to reprimand or scold severely (472) (888) (1014)
1221.	A claw **hammer**	a hammer with split end for extracting nails etc. (480) (680)
1222.	A claw **hammer** coat	a formal tail coat (US) (573) (834) (1505)
1223.	To get one's claws/**hooks** into someone	to entice or entrap him (often used in marital sense) (pej.) (617) (783) (1171)
1224.	To be in **clover**	to be well-off (359) (724) (1235)

1225.	A dumb **cluck**	a silly or brainless person (usually in reference to a woman) (415) (517) (1072)
1226.	To blow away the **cobwebs**	to reappraise something prior to starting afresh (1042) (1067)
1227.	To have one's **head** full of cobwebs	to be confused or dozy (1564) (1567)
1228.	A 'cobweb **science**'	his words to describe over-complicated metaphysical arguments – Adam Smith (273) (1254)
1229.	To slip the **collar**	to escape; to divorce (pej.) (446) (1284) (1346)
1230.	To be **cooped** up	to be confined (59) (468) (951)
1231.	To break **cover**	to be forced out of hiding (hunting term) (1172) (1560)
1232.	The **crawl**	a swimming stroke (148) (1000); a term often applied to travel on London's M25 'Motorway' (320) (1130) (1467)

1233.	A **creepy**-crawly	child's term for a nasty insect (1051) (1386) (1560)
1234.	A **pub** crawl	a visit to numerous public houses in succession (146) (1513) (1567) (a dog tied up: an unpaid 'pub' bill) (Aust. sl.)
1235.	One's **creature** comforts	requirements for an agreeable life-style (359) (724) (751)
1236.	To **croak**	to die (sl.) (902) (1111) (1418)
1237.	To **crop** up	to arise unexpectedly (842) (1473) (1550) (a crop: bird's gullct; handle of whip)
1238.	To chew the **cud**	to think things over cf. to ruminate (1202) (1388)
1239.	To **curb** someone	to restrain him (a curb: a strap under horse's jaw) (220) (237) (1435)
1240.	To **curry** favour	to seek advantage by flattery (to curry: to rub down a horse; to tan a hide) (132) (1147) (1319)

1241.	A **Derby**	a horse race (1547); a type of hat (resembling a 'bowler') (803) (1462)
1242.	A demolition **Derby**	a kind of stock-car race in which old cars are damaged or destroyed (282) (1392)
1243.	To **drench** an animal	to force it to take medicine (122)
1244.	To **earmark**	to set aside (money) for a special purpose (164) (1398)
1245.	'Don't put all your **eggs** in one basket'	advice to keep something in reserve; diversify (271) (824) cf. 'It serves me right for putting all my eggs in one bastard': Dorothy Parker, on her abortion.
1246.	You can't make an omelette without **cracking** eggs	there is no success without investment and sacrifice (338) (959)
1247.	The **curate's** egg	good but only in parts (1038) (1064)
1248.	To be left with egg on one's **face**	to be humiliated, especially in public (483) (1145) (1147)

1249.	An egg-**flip**	hot beer or wine mixed with an egg (also called an egg nog) (146)
1250.	A **good**/bad egg	a reliable/unreliable character (1037) (1556)
1251.	An egg-**head**	a scientific expert or 'boffin' (584) (1370)
1252.	To **lay** an egg	to flop or fail (US) (381) (388) (424)
1253.	To egg someone **on**	to urge or goad him on (204) (255) (1474)
1254.	'The vulgar boil, the learned **roast** an egg'	– Alexander Pope (1228)
1255.	'A kiss without a moustache is like an egg without **salt**'	– old Spanish saying
1256.	To try to **shave** an egg	to take on an impossible task (199) (303) (1117)
1257.	To teach your grandmother to **suck** eggs	to state the obvious to one who knows better than you (130) (373)
1258.	As **sure** as eggs is eggs	with the utmost certainty (possibly a corruption of 'x is x') (243) (373)

1259.	To **tread** on eggs	to proceed extra carefully (31) (77) (1675)
1260.	'...as **white** and hairless as an egg'	'On Julia's Legs' – Herrick 17th c. (1256) (1371)
1261.	To wear **ermine**	to wear robes adorned with a weasel-like fur – usually reserved to peers or judges (694) (1181)
1262.	To **farm** something out	to subcontract a job (1323) (1339)
1263.	To **feather**	to turn a blade edgeways eg. an oar (885); a neat method of joining two sheet metal edges (496)
1264.	**Feathers**	wispy fur or hair on legs of certain dogs and horses (121) (133)
1265.	To feather**bed** someone	to over-indulge him (730) (1203) (1435)
1266.	Feather**brained**	impractical; an 'airy-fairy' dreamer (432) (591) (1567)
1267.	A feather in one's **cap**	an honour or achievement (1474) (1546)
1268.	To be in **fine** feather	to be fit and healthy cf. to be on song (97) (1020) (1200)

1269.	All **fuss** and feathers	all show and display without any real substance (107) (522) (1114)
1270.	To **knock** someone down with a feather	to tell him something totally unexpected (319) (488) (678)
1271.	To feather one's own **nest**	selfishly promote or protect one's own interests (160) (917) (924)
1272.	To **ruffle** someone's feathers	to disturb his tranquillity (665) (1447)
1273.	To **smooth** someone's feathers	to calm him down; to win him round (131) (730)
1274.	To **spit** feathers	to be furious (301) (422) (513)
1275.	A feather**weight**	a lightweight boxer (approx. 54 to 57 kg) (335) (1003) (1047)
1276.	**White** feathers	a symbol of cowardice (341) (1508)
1277.	To put out **feelers**	to make discreet enquiries (5) (31) (900)
1278.	To rush one's **fences**	to be over hasty, increasing the risk of disaster (1326) (1383) (1437)

1279.	To be in a **flap**	to be flustered or agitated (788) (964) (966)
1280.	Fully-**fledged**	mature; ready to look after oneself (1474) (1555)
1281.	To **fleece** someone	to cheat him by taking without payment (392) (562) (1566)
1282.	A **flight** of fancy	a whimsical or romantic act that is out of character (415) (812)
1283.	The flight or **fight** reaction	a reaction induced by the body's increased adrenalin when under stress (861) (1389) (1511)
1284.	To **take** flight	to escape by the fastest means available (446) (1229) (1520)
1285.	**White** flight	reference to white parents withdrawing their children from schools containing black children cf. Jim Crow: segregation (US)
1286.	To be **flight**y	to be unreliable or unpredictable (312) (415) (812)

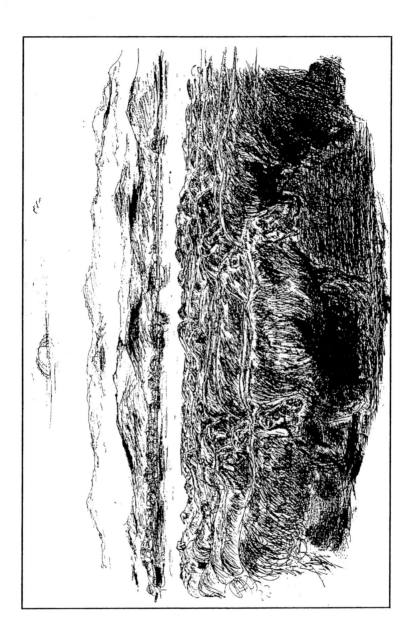

1287.	To **flock** somewhere	to go together in large numbers, so ensuring safety of the group (815) (975) (1331)
1288.	High**flown**	extravagant; unrealistically ambitious (pej.) (574) (1292)
1289.	To have a **flutter**	to place a small bet; to be mildly adventurous (271) (1433) (1443)
1290.	To **fly** in the face of	to rebel against or strongly contradict (617) (1184) (1299)
1291.	To fly off the **handle**	to lose one's temper (301) (587) (603)
1292.	The **higher** they fly, the harder they fall	lit. – a rather cynical interpretation of the law of gravity (cf. a high flyer: successful person) (23) (423) (1504)
1293.	'(Troubles) ...**flying** in flocks, are apt to perch capriciously'	*Barnaby Rudge* – Charles Dickens (82) (213) (461)
1294.	A flying **freehold**	a property owned (not rented) above ground floor level (English legal term) (1548)

1295.	Cannon-**fodder**	soldiers sent in large numbers to almost certain death (111) (644) (1028)
1296.	To return to the **fold**	to return to one's family and friends after a period of self-imposed absence (311) (451) (768)
1297.	**Foot** in mouth disease	a play on words meaning the tendency to say or do the wrong thing (by confusing the proper function of these body parts) (1301) (1359)
1298.	An old **fossil**	an elderly 'stick-in-the-mud'; an old-fashioned person (144) (217) (1361)
1299.	To make the **fur**/feathers fly	to arouse antagonisms; provoke a dispute (46) (309) (1356)
1300.	Kettle-**fur**	a 'hard-water', limescale deposit affecting kettles, water heaters etc.
1301.	To commit a **gaff**	to make a silly mistake (a gaff: spur of fighting cock) (1297) (1359)
1302.	A **Gallo**per	a wooden funfair horse; cf. a Charger: a large, flat dish (255) (1010)

1303.	Gallo**ping** (inflation)	a reference to normally steady and predictable things getting wildly out of control (587) (1417)
1304.	Fair **game**	a target which, in the opinion of the marksman (or critic), has invited attack (393) (564) (1368)
1305.	To be game **for** something	to be willing or in the mood for it (269) (793)
1306.	To be both poacher and game**keeper**	to be a hypocrite; to back both sides cf. to hedge one's bets (260) (375) (626)
1307.	A **Gill**	a quarter pint measure (first used for wines in 13th c.) (723) (757) (978)
1308.	To be **green** about the gills	to feel sick – especially seasick (54) (175)
1309.	To be **loaded** to the gills	to be completely inebriated (847) (945) (1085)
1310.	A **Gobble**	a rapid, straight putt into the hole (golf) (458) (1344)
1311.	To **gobble**	to eat fast and noisily (703); to emit a throat gurgle like a turkey cock (513) (1236)

1312.	**Gobble**degook/ gobbledygook	verbose and meaningless language (367) (634) (728)
1313.	To go to **ground**	to go into hiding (hunting term) (136) (836) (1536)
1314.	A **Grow**ler	a two-wheeled, horse-drawn taxi-cab (100) (1521)
1315.	'A series of **grunts**, snorts and expectorations'	from a contemporary account of Berlioz' 'Damnation of Faust' (184) (230) (1528)
1316.	To stick in one's **gullet**/craw/gizzard	different ways to express revulsion or irritation (715) (1317)
1317.	To make one's **hackles** rise	to anger one (hackles: the neck feathers of cock; neck fur of mammals) (665) (715) (1087)
1318.	A **halter**neck dress	dress that is almost strapless to give a 'bare-back' effect (58) (741) (790)
1319.	To eat out of someone's **hand**	to be compliant (132) (1145) (1240)
1320.	A **harness** cask	a wooden barrel for storing salted provisions on old ships (723)

1321.	To **die** in harness	to die working (236) (255) (266)
1322.	In **double** harness	in partnership (615) (1339)
1323.	To harness one's **resources**	to husband and exploit one's assets (1262) (1339)
1324.	**Hatches**, matches and despatches	births, marriages and deaths (411) (570) (955)
1325.	To **hatch** a plot	to think up a (nasty) scheme (816) (1538)
1326.	To give someone his **head**	to let him use his initiative (152) (1449) (1542)
1327.	To hide one's **head** in the sand	to be escapist; deliberately avoid involvement (in the belief one is not seen doing so) (517) (538)
1328.	To bring someone to **heel**	to use force to make him obey (417) (1348) (1463)
1329.	To be well-**heeled**	to be prosperous (origin: cock-fighting) (to heel: to arm) (23) (359)
1330.	The **herd** instinct	the idea of finding safety and anonymity in the crowd (444) (782) (815)

1331.	'Morality is the **herd** instinct in the individual'	– Friedrich Nietzsche 19th c. philosopher (815) (1287)
1332.	To be **hide**bound	to have fixed, narrow-minded ideas (144) (217) (1563)
1333.	To **find** neither hide nor hair of someone	to find no trace of him (1313) (1459)
1334.	To **nail** someone's hide	to dominate or control him (US) (220) (1328) (1435)
1335.	To **save** one's (own) hide	to run away, abandoning others (709) (848) (1229)
1336.	To **tan** the hide off someone	to give him a thorough beating (60) (201) (1545)
1337.	To be on a hid**ing** to nothing	to be in a hopeless, losing position (30) (82) (1486)
1338.	A **hive** of industry	a very busy place (596) (1362) (1491)
1339.	To **hive** off	to cream off the best; to subcontract business to others (547) (772) (1322)
1340.	To be **honey**combed	to be full of holes (228) (1017) (1069)

1341.	A **honker**	a pungent 'fart' (sl.) (1360); species of wild goose (Canada) (869)
1342.	To **hood**wink	to deceive; to trick the senses (origin: the hood used for hawking) (510) (1440) (1569)
1343.	To **hoof** it	to go on foot (283) (699); to run away (1229) (1335); to dance (less used) (629)
1344.	A **Hook**	a ball veering to left (Golf) (458) (1310); a ball played from off to on (Cricket) (326) (380) (390)
1345.	Hook **line** and sinker	completely (eg. to swallow a story hook line and sinker: to be completely taken in or deceived) (273) (1396) (1493)
1346.	To **sling** one's hook	to depart (sl.) (pej.) cf. to get off the hook: to escape (446) (1229) (1284)
1347.	A hook**er**	a prostitute (sl.) (785) (1131); a small Dutch or Irish sailing ship (526) (1458)
1348.	To jump through the **hoop**	to do as one is told (132) (1328) (1463)

1349.	A real **hoot**	a really amusing joke or incident (that makes one 'hoot' with laughter) (36) (528) (632)
1350.	Not caring two **hoots**/not giving a **hoot**	not caring at all; not in the least affected (145) (666) (709)
1351.	A hoot**er**	a motor horn (726); a long nose (186) (1414); an owl (541)
1352.	On the **horns** of a dilemma	faced with a very difficult choice or decision (33) (92) (808)
1353.	A **green**horn	a complete beginner (561) (799)
1354.	To horn **in**	to rush in boldly; to interrupt rudely (1207) (1423) (1532)
1355.	A **lant**horn	early type of lamp made of transparent horn, hence 'lantern' (299)
1356.	To **lock** horns with someone	to clash or disagree strongly with him (61) (94) (1299)
1357.	To **pull** one's horns in	to pull back or avoid contact (98) (1459)

1358.	To be horny	to be sexually aroused (sl.) (455) (1043)
1359.	A **howl**er	a stupid, 'eye-brow raising' mistake (364) (1297) (1301)
1360.	To **hum**	to stink (682) (865) (1341)
1361.	Humd**rum**	boringly ordinary (261) (1012) (1298)
1362.	To **make** things hum	to stir up great activity; to raise the pitch (1058) (1214) (1338)
1363.	To **hump**	to have sex (sl.) (285) (1043) (1408)
1364.	To **get**/have the hump	to be upset by something; to be mildly depressed (1422) (1426) (1427)
1365.	**Over** the hump	past the most difficult or dangerous part (5) (184) (1497)
1366.	'A woman... without a **positive** hump may marry whom she likes'	– Thackeray

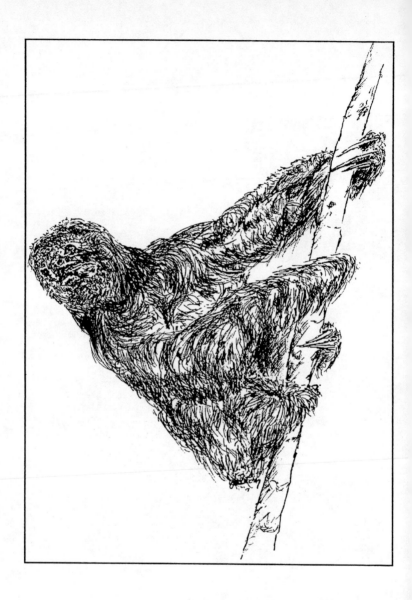

1367.	A **road** hump	a road bump designed to reduce traffic speed – increasingly seen in London. (Also called a 'sleeping policeman') (1130) (1456) (1494)
1368.	A **Hunt**er	a horse for hunting (393) (564); a type of pocket watch (similarly a half-hunter) (969)
1369.	A hunt**ing** carpet	a carpet depicting realistic hunting scenes (Persia)
1370.	The **Ivory** Dome	pompous term for the head (1251)
1371.	'An ivory **mischief**'	describing personal beauty – Theocritus 3rd c BC (1260)
1372.	To **tinkle** the ivories	to play the piano (823)
1373.	To live in an ivory **tower**	to live as an intellectual recluse (706) (1251) (1504)
1374.	To feel **jaded**	to feel worn out (a jade: a tired-out horse) (255) (1059) (1385)
1375.	A **Jock**	a Scotsman (usually used affectionately) (363) (1104) cf. a Kiwi: New Zealander

1376.	**Shock** jocks	radio chat show hosts who berate and belittle callers (149)
1377.	A jock**strap**	item of clothing worn by male athletes to support private parts (201) (881)
1378.	A disc jock**ey**	a person who verbally links CDs, records etc. 'live' or on radio (65)
1379.	The concrete **jungle**	generic term for a big city (856)
1380.	The law of the **jungle**	that the best adapted will survive (160) (856)
1381.	In at the **kill**	present at the vital moment (742) (1179) (1536)
1382.	To strain at the **leash**	to be very eager for action (269) (270) (1185)
1383.	To go hell for **leather**	to rush (leather: an alternative word for a saddle) (255) (1302) (1474)
1384.	A **Leather**jacket	the grub of a crane-fly (1386); a type of fish (Aust.) (379)
1385.	To be on one's last **legs**	to be ready to collapse from hunger or fatigue (1059) (1134) (1374)

1386.	A Daddy-long-**legs**	a crane-fly; field spider and certain other long-legged species (1233) (1384)
1387.	A **Leviathan**	anything huge and hard to control – Thomas Hobbes (615) (1068)
1388.	To **lick** one's wounds	to be rueful or reflective (659) (1202) (1238)
1389.	To be out on a **limb**	to be alone in an isolated or dangerous place (695) (1134) (1511)
1390.	To have nine **lives**	to be a survivor; to have a long run of good luck (7) (841) (1077)
1391.	A **Mews**	originally an enclosure for the Royal falcons; later on, stabling for horses; today a fashionable 'bijou' London residence (256) (424)
1392.	A **Moggy**/moggie	the affectionate name for an elderly cat or car (especially the Morris Minor) (282) (1242) (1518)
1393.	A **Mugger**	an Indian crocodile (1098); a street thief (10)

1394.	A **muzzle**-loader	a type of firearm (muzzle: open end of barrel) (93) (507) (1125)
1395.	To **muzzle** someone	to silence or censor him (874) (1523)
1396.	**Neck** and crop	completely (1345) (1493) (1546)
1397.	**Neck** and neck	running equal in a contest (1322) (1547)
1398.	A **nest**-egg	savings for an emergency, or special occasion (761) (1235) (1244)
1399.	To **foul** one's own nest	to damage one's own interests by acts committed too close to home (118) (620)
1400.	A nest of **saws**	a set of saw blades with one interchangeable handle (496) (1209)
1401.	A nest of **tables**	a set of tables fitting one within another to save space (1008)
1402.	To **nestle**	to settle closely (as a bird in a nest) (1183) (1203) (1265)

1403.	The **Net**	the international computer network ('Internet') (1525) (1539) (1541)
1404.	A neural **net**work	a computer programmed to mimic a biological function cf. 'Polly': world's first 'transgenic' sheep (818) (988)
1405.	To lead someone by the **nose**	to oblige him to follow and obey you (often used in sexual terms) (41) (137)
1406.	The **parson's** nose	a piece of flesh near the tail end of a cooked bird cf. the oyster: small, oval piece on back (372) (402) (449)
1407.	To **rub** someone's nose in it	to give him a sharp reminder to mend his ways (from the punishment often inflicted on dogs that 'miss the toilet') (118) (1528)
1408.	To get one's **oats**	to have sex (87) (491) (1363)
1409.	To be **off** one's oats	to lose one's appetite (because unwell) (441) (1416)

1410.	To sow one's **wild** oats	to seek one's pleasures while young (285) (430) (482)
1411.	To be put out to **pasture**	to be retired or laid-off (266) (1321)
1412.	A South**paw**	a left-handed boxer (or other athlete) (201) (1003)
1413.	'I am always sorry when any language is lost, because languages are the **pedigree** of nations'	– Dr Johnson (911) (993)
1414.	To keep one's **pecker** up	to stay cheerful (a Pecker: a nose) (sl.) (186) (794) (1351)
1415.	The peck**ing** order	the order of importance, rank or hierarchy (171) (362) (368)
1416.	To feel peck**ish**	to start to feel hungry (441) (1409); contrast: to peck at one's food (not hungry)
1417.	At full **pelt**	at full speed (to pelt: to hit hard and repeatedly) (968) (980) (1027)
1418.	To drop off one's **perch**	to die suddenly (411) (902) (1236)

1419.	To **pester**	to annoy by repeated irritating acts (715) (784) (1030)
1420.	A **pet** hate/aversion	a particular, personal dislike cf. a pet: a sulk or mood (235) (236)
1421.	Pett**ing**	kissing and fondling (but no further) (189) (1004) (1183)
1422.	To have the **pip**	to be depressed (pip: a disease of fowls) (88) (1364) (1427)
1423.	To **plough** through something	to push one's way through regardless (contrast: to plough an exam – to fail) (1207) (1354)
1424.	The **Pollen** Count	the number of grains of pollen per sq. cm. of microscopic slide (505) (975)
1425.	A 'first past the **post**' system	an electoral system where the winner takes all, in contrast to proportional representation (pol.) (1169) (1545)
1426.	To be **prey** to	to suffer from (239) (1364)
1427.	To **prey** on one's mind	to trouble or preoccupy one (88) (1089) (1422)

1428.	To **prick** up one's ears	to be on the alert (794) (1011) (1200)
1429.	A **prickly** customer	an awkward, hard to please person (prickly can also mean: over-sensitive) (83) (304) (835)
1430.	A **prowl** car	a police patrol car (US) cf. a prowler: a suspicious loiterer (10) (832)
1431.	To **put** someone out of his misery	to satisfy his curiosity or allay his fears (17) (290); to put down a sick pet (122)
1432.	A **Quack**	a bogus doctor (345) (581) (887)
1433.	A **racing** certainty	a sure thing; a complete gamble (ironic) (336) (1289) (1443)
1434.	An also-**ran**	a poor competitor; a second rate person (209) (249) (469)
1435.	To keep someone on a tight/long **rein**	to restrict/extend his activities (220) (237) (1239)
1436.	To take the **reins**	to assume control (5) (308) (645)

1437.	To **ride** for a fall	to behave so recklessly that one is destined for failure or disaster (693) (1278) (1383)
1438.	To give someone a **rough** ride	to treat him harshly or without consideration (145) (255) (1439)
1439.	To ride **roughshod** over someone	to ignore his welfare or wishes completely (roughshod: with nails deliberately left protruding) (145) (538) (1104)
1440.	To **take** someone for a ride	to swindle him (510) (1342)
1441.	A rid**er**	an addition to a document (559) (1032); a lover (US sl.) (455) (563)
1442.	Rid**ing** high	successful (359) (721) (724)
1443.	To have a lot **riding** on something	to gamble heavily upon a hoped for result (271) (1289) (1433)
1444.	To get a **rise** out of someone	to tease or provoke him into reacting (a fishing term) (665) (671)

1445.	To do a **roaring** trade	to conduct a thriving business (23) (87) (515)
1446.	To **rope** someone in	to oblige or persuade him to join in an activity, group etc. (201) (352) (727)
1447.	To **rub** someone up the wrong way	to do something calculated to irritate or upset him (665) (1272)
1448.	To **rule** the roost	to be in charge (171) (362) (368)
1449.	To have a good **run** for one's money	to receive good value or good treatment (origin: horse-riding) (152) (1542)
1450.	To **run** true to form	to perform as expected (form: refers to previous rankings, handicap etc. of racehorse) (984) (1474)
1451.	To make the runn**ing**	to set the pace or standard (268) (1488) (1546)
1452.	To **rustle** something up	to improvise something (often used for a 'scratch' meal or snack) (842) (1053) (1188)
1453.	To be **saddled** with someone	to have an unwanted guest or protégé (405) (907) (984)

1454.	To remove the **scales** from someone's eyes	to reveal the true state of things (787) (1150)
1455.	On the right **scent**	to be heading in the right direction; to have the right idea (518) (810) (1277)
1456.	To **screech** to a halt	to stop suddenly with one's brakes squealing (726) (920) (1499)
1457.	'Scruffts'	the annual show for mongrel dogs, run by the RSPCA (the official 'pedigree' show being Crufts) (103) (174) (698)
1458.	A **Shell**back	an old and experienced sailor (carrying boat on back like a turtle) (155) (1029) (1347)
1459.	To **go** into one's shell	to avoid contact with people (for fear of being hurt) (1327) (1333) (1373)
1460.	To shell **out**	to be obliged to pay for something, usually in a begrudging way (sl.) (1190) (1566)

1461.	The **Ship** of the Desert	the camel (on account of its undulating gait and fat (not water) – storing hump)
1462.	**Silks**	silk riding habit worn by jockeys (a Silk: Queen's Counsel – a senior barrister) (777) (984) (1241)
1463.	To **sit** up and beg	to plead obsequiously (usually used in sadistic or vengeful way – eg. 'I'll make him/her sit up and beg') (132) (1328) (1348)
1464.	To **slough** something off	to shed or get rid of something that has become useless or a burden (a snake sloughs off its dead skin) (848) (918)
1465.	To **snap**/to snarl at someone	to speak to him sharply or irritably (1019) (1099) (1290)
1466.	A **Snare** Drum	a side-drum (member of the percussion (membranophone) family). A snare: an attraction in sense that it beguiles or entraps (1121)

1467.	A **snarl** up	a traffic jam or similar situation (1232) (1367) (1494)
1468.	**Snout**	tobacco (sl.) (110) (442) (767)
1469.	To have one's **snout** in the trough	to be greedy; to accept illicit payments or favours (sl. pej.) (134) (262)
1470.	To **spin** a yarn	to tell a long, unlikely story (often to gain undue advantage) (156) (354)
1471.	'Poetry comes **finespun** to a mind at peace'	– Ovid (576) (805)
1472.	'Fame is the **spur**, that the clear spirit doth raise'	– Milton (1267) (1474)
1473.	On the spur of the **moment**	in a spontaneous, unplanned manner (68) (842) (1452)
1474.	To win **one's** spurs	to qualify; to win an honour or award cf. to spur on: to encourage (204) (255) (1267)
1475.	A **squawk** box	a public address system cf. a bull-horn: a loud-hailer (1173)

1476.	To eat everything but the **squeak**	to leave nothing (reference to the parts of a pig) (508) (703) (749)
1477.	**Stalking**	the action of a man unlawfully trailing a woman (711) (744) (1430) cf. to fox: to pursue stealthily (Aust.)
1478.	**Stamp**ing grounds	a habitual venue or meeting place (origin: the stamping of horses' hooves) (313) (965)
1479.	**Star**-Gazey Pie	a mackerel dish served with their heads pointing upwards (379) (1146)
1480.	To draw someone's **sting**	to render him harmless (122) (407) (1142)
1481.	To sting **someone**	to cheat or overcharge him (392) (1281)
1482.	To have a sting in the **tail**	capable of retaliating or giving one a nasty reminder at the last moment (582) (795) (970)
1483.	To **take** the sting out of something	to make it more palatable or acceptable (1142)

1484.	A **Stirrup** Cup	a parting drink (originally limited to departing riders, now used more widely) (121)
1485.	If you tell home truths, keep one foot in the **stirrup**	malicious gossip has a habit of catching up with its author (43) (1036)
1486.	To draw the short **straw**	to be committed to perform an unpleasant task or duty (82) (331) (1337)
1487.	A man of **straw**	a penniless person (used by lawyers to mean someone not worth suing) (150) (163) (821)
1488.	To take a thing in one's **stride**	to do it effortlessly (1451) (1474)
1489.	'Get **stuffed**!'	very impolite form of 'get lost!'sl. (524) (1346)
1490.	To be **stung** to the quick	to be deeply wounded or offended (usually by hurtful words) (888) (926) (1014); 'quick': sensitive flesh under nail or skin
1491.	To **swarm**/be aswarm with	reference to large numbers of moving creatures (pej.) (975) (1060) (1287)

1492.	In the **swim**	conversant or familiar with (French: 'in the bath') (611) (947)
1493.	In one fell **swoop**	all at a single stroke (from the swooping of hawks) (1345) (1396)
1494.	A **tail**-back	a long traffic queue caused by an accident, roadworks etc. (1130) (1367) (1467)
1495.	Ragtag and **bob**tail	the common people; the rabble (pej.) (595) cf. grey mice: ordinary Russian people (pej.)
1496.	To **chase** one's own tail	to go in circles and so get nowhere; to do something futile (165) (218) (358)
1497.	The tail-**end** of something	the last part or moment (579) (1365)
1498.	A tail**gate**	a part of a vehicle at the rear (292) cf. a trunk: a car boot (US)
1499.	To tailgate someone	to drive dangerously close behind his vehicle (prevalent in France) (726) (920) (1456)

1500.	Able to make neither **head** nor tail of something	completely perplexed or baffled by it (338) (1496)
1501.	'**Heads** or Tails?'	reference to the age-old practice of deciding a question by the toss of a coin (33)
1502.	'Calling a tail a **leg** don't make it a leg'	Abraham Lincoln (attrib.) (641) (739) (750)
1503.	With one's tail between one's **legs**	in a defeated or deflated manner (123) (343)
1504.	'Sit we upon the highest throne in the world, yet sit we only upon our **own** tail'	– Montaigne (423) (1292) (1373)
1505.	Tail**s**	man's formal evening wear; the parts of stone steps that are built into the wall (834) (1222)
1506.	To put **salt** on someone's tail	to catch or put him out of action (after the old adage of catching birds in this fashion) (220) (861) (1549) cf. old birds are not caught with chaff
1507.	To go into a tail**spin**	to lose control (a flying term) (112) (467) (884)

1508.	To **turn** tail	the act just prior to running away – usually followed by the words 'and run' (52) (343) (1276)
1509.	'Heads **I win**, tails you lose'	a gloss on the usual formula to mean 'a foregone conclusion' – with the inference of cheating or foul play (300) (325)
1510.	To show one's **teeth**	to demonstrate one's power; to give a final warning (1465)
1511.	At the end of one's **tether**	pushed to the limits of one's patience; on the verge of losing one's temper (386) (1134) (1507)
1512.	To be at one another's **throats**	to fight savagely (in mortal combat, dogs target the throat) (34) (1517)
1513.	On the **tiles**	to be out enjoying the night-life (orig.: cats crying for company from the rooftops) (460) (540) (961)
1514.	A **Tom**boy	rather dated term for a girl emulating fashion and behaviour of a boy (72)

1515.	With one's **tongue** hanging out	parched with thirst – (from action of dog to lower body heat) (104) (758)
1516.	To set the **tongues** wagging	to start people gossiping (43) (495) (813)
1517.	To fight **tooth** and claw	to wage all-out war, using all the weapons available (34) (1512)
1518.	To be **long** in the tooth	to be elderly (153) (208) (1392)
1519.	To work tooth and **nail**	to slave at, or put one's soul into, a job of work (89) (266) (792)
1520.	To make **tracks**	to get moving (and in the case of an animal, leave tracks for the hunter) (294) (1212) (1284)
1521.	A **trap**	a two-wheeled spring carriage (1181); a curve in drain-pipe (1314); a dark volcanic rock
1522.	The **poverty** trap	the dilemma of losing state benefits because of a small rise in one's income (821)
1523.	To **shut** one's trap	to stop talking (sl.) (874) (1395)

1524.	The **tender** trap	love (871) (1183) (1421)
1525.	To **trawl** the Net	to search or 'surf' for information on Internet (1403) (1539) (1541)
1526.	To go to the top of one's **tree**	to reach the pinnacle of one's profession, become a 'captain of industry' etc. (171) (368) (1267)
1527.	To be out of one's **tree**	to be insane – because out of one's normal (mental) habitat (426) (532) (786)
1528.	'I believe I have **trodden** in some'	expressing his opinion upon the music of Stockhausen – Sir Thomas Beecham (the word 'some' referring of course to dog mess) (1092) (1315) (1407)
1529.	To do several things on the **trot**	to perform several tasks easily and virtually at the same time (with the idea of a horse's legs moving at a steady pace in diagonal pairs) (890) (1473)
1530.	To **have** the trots	to be suffering from diarrhoea (similar to: 'to have the runs' and so needing no further explanation) (125) (1528)

1531. To trot something **out** — to recite it effortlessly; to display a talent (from trotting out a horse to show it off) (149)

1532. 'Till savage Ruskin he sticks his **tusk** in' — a complaint against the art critic by a Royal Academician (69) (603) (1354)

1533. A **tweeter** — a type of loudspeaker (high frequency) (65) (1376) (1378)

1534. A **Twitcher** — an avid birdwatcher (the term apparently stems from rapid head movements of the watchers) (655) (1080) ('I am not a word botcher': Rev. Spooner)

1535. To **twitter** (on) — to chatter inanely, or giggle – similar to the wittering of birds (307) (535) (1571)

1536. 'The unspeakable in full pursuit of the **uneatable**' — 'The English country gentleman galloping after a fox' (from *A Woman of No Importance* – Oscar Wilde) (742) (1179) (1381)

1537. An **urchin** — countryman's name for a hedgehog (814)

1538.	A **web** of intrigue	a secret plot or conspiracy; a complex mystery (816) (1325)
1539.	A Web-**Site**	an address on the Internet System cf. a domain (1403) (1525) (1541)
1540.	'Oh, what a **tangled** web we weave, when first we practice to deceive'	practice improves us, especially in the art of lying: Lochinvar – Sir Walter Scott (710) (763)
1541.	The **World** Wide Web	denoting the territory of the Internet System (1403) (1525) (1539)
1542.	To be given a fair crack of the **whip**	to receive a fair chance (152) (1449)
1543.	To have the whip **hand**	to be in command; to have a controlling influence (171) (368) (1185)
1544.	A whip-**round**	a collection of money (usually among work colleagues to buy wedding, birthday or leaving present) (761)

1545.	A **Three** Line Whip	a Notice requiring party members to vote in Parliament according to its terms (1123) (1169) (1425)
1546.	To **win** hands down	to win convincingly or outright (from a rider lowering his reins at the end of a race) (249) (1219) (1474)
1547.	To **win** by a whisker	to win by the narrowest possible margin – certainly a photo-finish (1241) (1397) (1474)
1548.	A **wing**	the lateral member of an aircraft or motor vehicle (366) (884); an extension to a large house (1294)
1549.	To **clip** someone's wings	to limit his freedom or scope of activity (a bird with clipped wings cannot fly) cf. to wing: to graze with bullet (122) (1506)
1550.	To wing **it**	to improvise (origin: a stand-in actor having to be prompted from the wings); to escape (842) (1237) (1473)
1551.	'Friendship is **Love** without his wings'	– Byron

1552.	A wing-**nut**	a type of nut (mechanical) (1006) (1090)
1553.	On a wing and a **prayer**	with no real chance of survival (believed to be a flying term – Second W. War) (30) (101) (418)
1554.	Wing**s**	the parts of a theatre at either side of stage (830) (1007) cf. flies: space over the stage
1555.	To **spread** one's wings	to be adventurous (1280) (1474)
1556.	To **sprout** wings	to perform kind deeds (thereby being seen as angelic) (877) (949)
1557.	To **take** someone under one's wing	to protect him – as a bird safe – guards its young (1203) (1265) (1402)
1558.	Wing-**tips**	a shoe-fashion reminiscent of wings from their shape (US) (277) (963) (982)
1559.	To **wait** in the wings	to await one's turn; to be ready to help (a theatrical term) (1007)

1560.	To come out of the **woodwork**	reference to something nasty or unexpected coming to light (origin: wood-boring insects) (801) (1121)
1561.	A **Woofer**	a type of loudspeaker (low frequency) (65) (1376) (1378)
1562.	All **wool** and a yard wide	the genuine article; of finest quality (66) (670) (973)
1563.	**Dyed**-in-the-wool	fixed in one's ways; reactionary (217) (1194) (1332)
1564.	Wool**gathering**	day-dreaming; absentmindedness (277) (1227)
1565.	To **get** in someone's wool	to irritate him; to get on his nerves (or 'in his hair') (665) (715) (1316)
1566.	'To **go** for wool and come back shorn'	advice to stay peacefully in the safety of one's home – Miguel Cervantes (562) (736) (1281)
1567.	Woolly-**headed**	seeing the world in a haze eg. through excessive drink (274) (1227) (1266)

1568.	To **lose** one's wool	to become bad-tempered and aggressive (422) (599) (1274)
1569.	To **pull** the wool over someone's eyes	to deceive him by concealing the facts (57) (756) (787)
1570.	**Wild** and woolly	untamed and uncivilised (617) (1205)
1571.	To **yap** on	to chatter on annoyingly (307) (535)
1572.	Under the **yoke**/yoked	enslaved; married (very pej.) (211) (681)
1573.	'The most heterogeneous ideas are **yoked** by violence together'	– Dr Johnson (160) (696) (1205)
1574.	A **zoo** event	an unexplained astronomical happening (162) (1080)
1575.	**Zoo**morphic	attributing the form or nature of an animal to something else ie. an 'animal saying'